Ace of the Iron Cross

Ace of the Iron Cross

ERNST UDET
Oberleutnant, Imperial German Air Service

Edited by

STANLEY M. ULANOFF
Colonel, U.S.A.R.

Translated by

RICHARD K. RIEHN

AIR COMBAT CLASSICS

ARCO PUBLISHING, INC.
NEW YORK

First Arco Edition, First Printing, 1981

Published by Arco Publishing, Inc.
219 Park Avenue South, New York, N.Y. 10003

Copyright © 1970 by Stanley M. Ulanoff

Library of Congress Cataloging in Publication Data

Udet, Ernst, 1896–1941.
　　Ace of the Iron Cross.

　　(Air combat classics)
　　Translation of Mein Fliegerleben.
　　Reprint of the 1970 ed. published by Doubleday, New York.
　　1. Udet, Ernst, 1896–1941. 2. European War, 1914–1918—Personal narratives, German. 3. Air pilots—Germany—Biography. I. Ulanoff, Stanley M. II. Title.
[TL540.U3A313 1981]　940.4'4943'0924 [B]　80-26156
ISBN 0-668-05161-2 (Cloth Edition)
ISBN 0-668-05163-9 (Paper Edition)

Printed in the United States of America

ACKNOWLEDGMENTS

I must express my gratitude to fellow "Cross and Cockade" member Richard K. Riehn, who did a magnificent job of translating, from the original German, Ernst Udet's exciting, dramatic autobiography, *Mein Fliegerleben* (which has been retitled *Ace of the Iron Cross*). Dick Riehn's translation is the first in the English language of this epic "Air Combat Classic."

I am particularly grateful to the Magazine and Book Branch of the U.S. Air Force Office of Public Affairs and to Duane Reed, Betsy Kysely, and Betty Fogler of the U.S. Air Force Academy Library for their invaluable assistance.

I must also acknowledge the contribution of the late Lew Glaser and Howard Rieder of Revell, Inc.; and Joe Phelan, another "Cross and Cockade" buddy, who furnished their fine three-view drawings of First World War aircraft.

My appreciation goes as well to my ever-helpful friends at the Bryant Library in Roslyn, and the Great Neck Library, both of New York; and the libraries in Lenox and Stockbridge, Massachusetts.

Thanks to my good friend and fellow author, Bill Hess, for the photos he sent me, and to Tom Abbott and the wonderful Xerox copier that duplicated the entire original volume without damage to it.

STANLEY M. ULANOFF
Editor

CONTENTS

LIST OF PHOTOGRAPHS

15. *The American, Lieutenant Wanamaker, wounded on a stretcher, after being shot down.*

16. *From then on, my aircraft was named* Lo.

17. *Udet's quarters with the Richthofen group.*

18. *Bodenschatz, Udet, Bolle.*

19. *Goering, Von Wedel, Schulte-Frohlinde.*

20. *Back with the* staffel *on June 28, 1918, after bailing out. On the right: Drekmann.*

21. *Goering, last C.O. of the Richthofen group.*

22. *Eddie Rickenbacker, the most successful surviving American fighter pilot.*

23. *René Fonck, the most successful surviving French fighter pilot.*

24. *William A. Bishop, the most successful surviving British ace.*

25. *In Los Angeles, Roscoe Turner gives me the final aerial note from the student from Ontario.*

26. *U 4 of the Udet Aircraft Company in South America, 1923.*

27. *Landing on the Moenchjoch in Switzerland.*

28. *In the African interior.*

29. *Schneeberger and Suchocky examine the damage done by the lioness.*

30. *National Air Races in Los Angeles.*

31. *The foreign team in Cleveland: De Bernardi (Italy); Orlynsky (Poland); Al Williams (U.S.); Udet; Cubita (Czechoslovakia).*

32. *Arctic night.*

33. *Our expeditionary ship in Nugaitsiak.*

LIST OF DRAWINGS

INTRODUCTION

Oberleutnant* Ernst Udet was the leading surviving ace of the Imperial German Military Air Service in the Great War of 1914–18, and his sixty-two victories placed him second only to Manfred von Richthofen, the "Red Baron." He also had the distinction of being the youngest German ace, having entered the service in 1914 at eighteen years of age. By the signing of the Armistice in November 1918 he had reached the ripe old age of twenty-two.

Udet, who began the war as a motorcyclist, transferred to the air service and became a pilot. He flew as an enlisted man because the Germans, like the French and English, did not necessarily give commissions to their pilots. (The United States, on the other hand, awarded officer's commissions to all of its pilots. Most of the Americans who flew with the Lafayette Flying Corps held the French ranks of sergeant or corporal, but received commissioned ranks in the U. S. Air Service when this nation entered the war.)

Later on Udet, too, became an officer, and by the end of the war commanded a fighter squadron in the "Red Baron's" elite Jagdgeschwader No. 1.† Before joining Von Richthofen, he was in command of Jasta 37,‡ and under the Baron's tutelage took the reins of Jasta 11. He was a stunt pilot and made movies in Africa and the Arctic during the 1920s and '30s. During World War II he became a general in the Luftwaffe. Unfortunately, he did not get along with Hermann Goering, his former fellow fighter pilot of the Richthofen Geschwader

* First lieutenant.
† Fighter Group No. 1.
‡ Short for Jagdstaffel (Fighter Squadron) 37.

who had become the Nazi chief of the Luftwaffe and who forced Udet to commit suicide in 1941.

In his younger days, however, he was a happy-go-lucky, daring fellow. His First War Fokker D VII had diagonal red and white stripes on the top wing, his girl friend "Lo's" name on the sides of the fuselage, and the tail bore the taunting inscription *"Du doch nicht!!"*—"Definitely not you!!"—as a dare to any Allied flier skillful enough to get behind him to place him in a vulnerable position. One intrepid fellow apparently did just that, because Udet was forced to bail out of his aircraft in a parachute to save his skin. This was a luxury not afforded to Allied pilots, who either had to jump, to their deaths, without the aid of 'chutes, or remain with their machines to burn up with them or crash to the earth below.

But the above unpleasantness aside, Ernst Udet was a carefree, happy, if not innocent, young man who was actually "gun shy" on his first encounter with a French machine, when he fled in the opposite direction. But during his stunt pilot days he earned the nickname of the "Flying Fool."

It is indeed regrettable that his Nazi masters forced his trigger finger with the gun at his temple.

Ace of the Iron Cross is a brand new translation of Ernst Udet's *Mein Fleigerleben*. It tells not only of his adventures in the First World War, including his breathtaking, dramatic battle with the legendary French hero, Georges Guynemer, but also of his experiences as an aircraft manufacturer, his racing and stunt flying in Argentina and the United States, and his exciting interludes in Africa and the Arctic.

With the possible exception of the small last chapter, which may have been written or dictated by the Nazis, *Ace of the Iron Cross* is an exciting, authentic "Air Combat Classic."

STANLEY M. ULANOFF, *Editor*

Ace of the Iron Cross

FLIGHT OVER ENEMY TERRITORY

As I step into our room, Niehaus' words reach me at the door. "Udet, report to Lieutenant Justinius right away. He's sent for you twice already."

I straighten my cap, cockade in line with the bridge of the nose, and walk along the gray barracks hall. The other flight cadets are returning from a hike and clank past me with their field packs and carbines.

What could Justinius want from me? Maybe he found out who sprayed gasoline under the tail of the captain's dog. Would he be bothered about that? After all, he's merely on detached service, here in Darmstadt, to pick out pilots for his outfit. He has no business meddling with the internal affairs of the replacement unit.

I knock at a narrow door with a small white card: "Lt. Justinius," and enter.

Justinius, in shirt sleeves, is lying on his bunk. His uniform coat is draped over the back of a chair, and the ribbon of the Iron Cross is prominent in the second button hole. Outside the open window a hot summer day gleams.

I stand at attention.

"Sit down, Udet," says Justinius, while sticking out a leg to sweep a stack of newspapers off the chair onto the floor.

I sit down and look at him expectantly.

"How old are you?" he begins without preamble.

"Nineteen, *Herr Leutnant.*"

"Hm," he grunts, "a bit young."

"But I'll be twenty soon," I add quickly, "next year in April."

Laugh crinkles form around his eyes. "Well, then hurry up," he says. "And how did you get into flying?"

I begin to realize what he is after.

"Near the end of 'fourteen I was discharged as a motorcycle volunteer," I reply eagerly, "and immediately reported to a pilot replacement unit. But they wouldn't take me."

"Why?"

"Because I was too young then," I admit reluctantly.

Justinius smiles again. "Then what?"

"After that I took training as a private pilot at the Otto Works in Munich.

"At your own expense?"

"My father paid two thousand marks and furnished a bathroom for Mr. Otto."

I want to continue, but Justinius cuts me short with a wave of the hand. He raises himself, chin propped on an elbow, and scrutinizes me with his hard, blue eyes. "Would you like to come with me as my pilot?" he asks.

Although I was expecting it by this time, I blushed just the same. For joy. Because Justinius is a fine fellow. "Damn snappy dog," the flight trainees said of him.

"Certainly, *Herr Leutnant*," I trumpeted against all the rules of form. He gave me a friendly nod.

"All right."

I stand up and do my bit. At the door he calls me back. "Are you free this evening?" As I answer yes, he says: "Then we'll have to celebrate our wedding, 'Emil.'"

"Yes sir, *Leutnant* 'Franz.'" With him I risked such an answer. In pilots' language, "Emil" was the name of the pilot, "Franz" was the observer. But I did not yet quite dare to call him just plain "Franz."

We return toward morning. I have long overstayed my pass, and Justinius drapes his officer's cape over my shoulders so I can get past the sentries.

Next morning, during training flights over the Griessheim flats, I almost cracked up. Preoccupied with the previous night's conversations with Justinius, I neglected to give my student a well-timed rap on his flying cap. This fellow, a tall, fat, delicatessen dealer, always flattened out too soon when coming in. So, at the critical moment, I would give him a reminder with my walking stick. This time, he barely got it in the nick of time.

Fourteen days have passed since I joined *Flieger-Abteilung* 206 at Heiligkreuz. Every day, Justinius and I make several flights. Our usual job is ranging the artillery of our sector. Thus we almost always have the same landscape below us: the Three Ears, the black and white lakes which, shaded by the slopes of Vosges, blink up at us like pools of molten lead.

Only on occasion do we reach farther afield. Once we went so far that we could see the round cap of the church steeple of Dié winking at us across the ridges of the hills. We had been motorcyclists then, back when the war started. Was it only nine months ago, or nine years? Five of us went out there right at the start, in August, but only three returned home in December. One was shot dead by the French; the other took his own life, because he could not cope with the war and with the hard demands of the service. How far all this lies in the past. I sometimes think it must have happened in some other life.

At times, we also encounter the enemy. But we in observation aircraft do not harm each other. We have hardly any weapons aboard, and both sides are aware of this. Thus we pass like ships at sea. With the beginning of fall, the air war becomes tougher. At first, steel darts were dropped from the aircraft on the troops below. Now, bombs have been made whose effect is almost equal to that of shell bursts. In order to impress the enemy forcefully with the capabilities of this new invention, a bombing raid with all available aircraft is mounted against Belfort on September 14.

Justinius and I fly along. It is a gray day, and we don't break through the cloud cover until we reach thirty-five hundred meters. Up here it's wondrously quiet; the air is almost still. Our Aviatik B with the 120-Mercedes glides along like a swan. Justinius frequently leans over the side to look at the ground visible through gaps in the cloud cover.

Suddenly, a metallic ping, as though a piano wire had snapped. In the next moment, the machine lists to the left, goes into a spin, and descends into the clouds. Over the back rest of the front seat, Justinius' face appears pale and questioning. I shrug my shoulders. I myself don't know yet what has happened. All I know is that I must step onto the right rudder with all the strength I have and turn the wheel until my hands ache. We fall a thousand meters before the aircraft flattens out again. It still lists, but it doesn't spin any more, and we can hope to glide to the ground. To the ground—this means capture! We are still at least fifteen kilometers short of the German lines.

Justinius points at the right upper wing. I see that the shackle anchoring a guy wire must have torn. The wire flaps in the wind and the air pressure billows the wing upward. We are gliding on an easterly course, toward Switzerland. Off and on, I gun the engine to stall loss of altitude. Then the machine turns on its side again, more and more, and I fear we will spin again. I shut the throttle.

We break out of the clouds above Montbéliard. The altimeter registers eighteen hundred meters, and the Swiss border is still twelve kilometers off. It seems impossible to reach.

Justinius stands up and slowly climbs out of his cockpit onto the right wing, feeling his way to the center strut. There he lets himself down, his legs dangling in the air. My heart beats in my throat from just watching him. We are sixteen hundred meters up. I open the throttle again, and the machine again tips to the side. The counterbalance given by Justinius is noticeable, but not sufficient.

I won't be able to hold the wheel like this for long. I feel my arms beginning to tremble. I wave at Justinius. In doing so, my cramped arm flaps back and forth like a piston torn loose.

"Come," I shout, "come." The "sir" and all other amenities are forgotten.

And Justinius comes. Slowly he creeps across the slanting wing plane and climbs back into the cockpit.

Several powerful blows shake the aircraft, the thin wooden back of the observer's seat is splintered. Two hands appear, two bleeding hands, scraped by splintered wood, wave through the air and grab hold of the wheel. Justinius is there, Justinius is helping me!

His face, pale under the tan and covered with the perspiration of exertion, momentarily appears above the opening. "We have to hold out, boy," he shouts, "to Switzerland." We are one thousand meters up and still eight kilometers from the border.

The ground below is entirely untouched by the war—villages with red roofs, bedded in the juicy green of fruit trees, the living chessboard of the fields.

There! Right through the middle of the fields runs the barbed wire, the barrier the Swiss have erected to keep out our deserters. At an altitude of six hundred meters, we cross the border near St. Dizier.

"Switzerland," I shout forward. Justinius' face again appears over the shattered back of the observer's seat. "On to Germany!" he shouts back.

Gas, glide, gas, glide. We skim over the landscape at low altitude. In the hamlets, people stop on the streets and gape with open mouths. This must be Courtremaiche. There's Vendlincourt. And then—again barbed wire—the German border!

We land on a freshly plowed field, jump out of the aircraft, and look at each other—and suddenly it takes hold of us like a drunken fit. There is no more Lieutenant Justinius and Private Udet, only "Franz" and "Emil," two kids hopping about like Sioux Indians dancing around a stake, picking up clods of dirt and throwing them at each other as though they were snowballs. Our landing has been observed, and people come running across the field. We regain our composure. Justinius asks a cyclist to go to the nearest town to phone Heiligkreuz.

The crowd of curious onlookers grows steadily while we pace up and down along the airplane. Justinius claps me on the shoulder. "You know what?" he says. "We'll let them make us a new shackle here and fly back under our own steam." A great idea.

The blacksmith of Winkel looks the thing over with wrinkled brow. "In three hours you'll have a new one," he says. We walk back to the airplane and the townsfolk follow us as though we were tightrope walkers.

A gray car comes speeding along the road and stops. An officer climbs out, and the crowd around us opens a passage. The officer, an air staffer, comes toward us.

Justinius makes his report, and the staff officer shakes hands with both of us. "You did a great job, boys." He walks over to the plane. "And where's the damage?"

Justinius, beaming: "Already being fixed, *Herr* Hauptmann."

The staff officer whips around: "What?"

He is beside himself. Such a material flaw must be handed

over to the testing commission. We should have known as much!

We climb into his car and drive to the village smithy, silently and dejectedly. The smith meets us at the door, the craftsman's satisfaction on his face. "Here." He hands us the new shackle.

"And where's the old one?" The staffer's question sounds quite sharp. The smith's broad thumb points backward over his shoulder toward the yard. The gate is open and one can see a manure heap piled high. On top of it chicken cackle in the sunshine. "Well, go look for it, then," the air staffer snaps at me. I walk into the yard and Justinius comes along, remaining at my side.

The shackle is easy to find; it lies on top of the heap. We rinse it off under the pump and bring it to the captain. He looks at it and shoves it into his pocket. The smith is paid, and we climb in. We are to ride along to Mülhausen. The smith looks after us, shaking his head.

The air staff officer still hasn't cooled down. "Blockheads," he grunts to himself. Then, with a shrug, he turns to us and suddenly becomes quite gracious:

"You must excuse my agitation, gentlemen, but just today two comrades of your unit, Lieutenant Winter and Sergeant Preiss, had an accident. Crashed on the Hartmannsweilerkopf. Probably due to the same material flaw. Both are dead!"

A shadow falls over our elation.

A week later, the daily bulletin reads: "Lieutenant Justinius has received the Iron Cross First Class, Private Udet the Iron Cross Second Class. Because they have preserved an aircraft for the Fatherland."

Another bombing raid has been scheduled. This time, it is to go against some fortified nests in the Vosges Mountains.

The flight might be of greater duration, so the fuel tanks have been filled to the top. Beyond that, we also carry two machine guns. French fighters are said to be roaming in the area. One even speaks of Pégoud.*

At the start the machine lifts off with effort, like a swan whose fattened belly is too weighty for its wings. The machine guns, the full tanks, the new radio set, bombs—all this pulls downward. I go into a wide, climbing turn. Below us the airfield, the dull green of the pasture, the flat gray of the tents. We climb slower than usual—one hundred meters—two hundred.

Just over the tents I bank the machine into a curve. She doesn't straighten out again but droops by the left wing. I kick to the right—to no avail—the rudder no longer responds. Speed loss! A moment later, the aircraft noses down and speeds toward the ground in a tight spiral.

"Justinius," I think, "for God's sake, Justinius is lost. When we hit the ground, the engine will bash to the rear and squeeze off his legs."† I yank the stick to my chest, kick to the right, kick, kick. . . . Before me, an arm reaches out of the observer's cockpit and takes hold of the tension rod. With a jerk, Justinius pulls himself out of his cockpit and sits on the backrest of his seat. "Udet," he screams, "Udet— Uuuu . . ." Gurgles, crashing, everything goes black . . . in my skull, a mighty bell drones. . . .

And then, after a long time, a voice: "Still 'live, Herr Udet?" Above me looms the thick face of Behrend, my mechanic, creased with worry.

Then, four strong arms grab me and pull me out of the maze of wood and steel. My knee is stuck fast; it hurts terribly. They must first bend back the steel piping.

* An early French stunt flier and wartime ace.
† The observer sat forward of the pilot.

"Where is Justinius?"

Behrend points to the grass. There he lies, on his back, face up and eyes closed.

"Dead?" I shout.

Behrend, soothing: "No, no, he's tough. He already asked about you."

They pick me up, two and two, and carefully deposit me close alongside Justinius. For quite a while I lie motionless. Above me, the pale blue sky; below me the moist, cool grass and the solid, living earth. Slowly I turn my head toward Justinius. He still keeps his eyes closed. A thin line of blood runs from his lips across his chin.

Perhaps . . . ?

But there comes a hand across the grass toward me, just as the hand of a sick person feels its way over the bed sheets. Carefully, I hold mine out and feel his pressure, the good, hard pressure of a friend's hand. We don't say a word.

"Lieutenant Justinius . . . Justinius, my comrade!"

Behind us, the mechanics are working on our machine. "Well, were they lucky the bombs didn't go off," I hear Behrend's voice. Then the medics come and place us on stretchers and shove us into a car like loaves of bread. At the hospital in Colmar we are separated.

Justinius, who was thrown clear on impact, suffered abrasions and contusions. My knee has bursitis in the joint. A thick bag hangs there, and I'm to be laid up for quite a while.

After ten days I am allowed up for the first time to hobble through the hallways. During the entire period, I've had no mail from home, and none of my buddies has visited me. It seems as though I've been lost to the rest of the world.

I simply must return to my unit. I hold out for another ten days, then I inform the doctor. He raises his eyebrows in surprise. But, after all, I'm not in the infantry and it's not his leg. So he hands me my discharge papers for the next day.

The first one I run into on the airfield is a buddy with whom I've often traveled on leave to Colmar, a pilot of our unit. I hail him and he greets me with some embarrassment and quickly moves on. It could be a coincidence, but the three standing in front of the large tent turn their backs quite ostensibly.

Finally, I run into Behrend. He scratches his head suggestively and pulls me off into a corner between the tents. It's a damned story. As soon as we came down, the C.O. had grabbed the phone and called the air staff officer. He blew up quite a storm: Private Udet had just now crashed due to wild maneuvering. He requests that Udet be immediately relieved from duty and severely punished. "Most severe punishment!" he screamed. Everyone in the orderly room heard it. My replacement is already here, and I can pick up my papers. I've been transferred back to the flight park at Neubreisach.

Behrend weighs his head in sorrow. I thank him, pick up my papers at the orderly room, and limp to my quarters. In the afternoon I sit on the sofa, the injured leg stretched out. My landlady kneels in front of me, packing my suitcase under my instruction. Her face is swollen from crying, and from time to time she gives out a deep sigh. I was always one of her good tenants, and I never deducted the insect powder from the rent.

There is a knock on the door. Justinius stands on the threshold. He comes toward me and, as I attempt to get up, pushes me back into the green plush.

"Ease up, shorty," he says in a friendly voice, "that's the way it goes, up and down. After all, we're in the flying service."

He pats me on the shoulder and presses a large box of

cigarettes into my hand. Then he leaves. He has to take off immediately on an observation flight with my successor.

I never saw Justinius again. He fell in '17 on the Western Front as a fighter pilot.

I arrived at the flight park at Neubreisach after dark. "Aha, there we have the gentleman who turned the curve," says the sergeant. The clerks are grinning. Since it's late, I am sent to the supply room to draw bedding. During this night I can't sleep a wink.

Next morning, the flight trainees fall in outside in the yard. I have to stay in the barracks. Then, somebody comes to get me.

The captain stands in front of the formation and looks toward me with dark and threatening mien. I walk on rubber legs.

"About face!" he commands as I stand six paces in front of him. A hundred pairs of eyes stare at me with cold curiosity.

"Look at him!" thunders the voice behind me. "This is the dumbhead who, through careless flying, has cost the Fatherland a new and valuable machine and seriously jeopardized his observer's life."

The pilot trainees look at me as though I had just committed patricide.

There is a rustle of paper, and the captain reads in cool and businesslike fashion:

"Pfc. Udet is to be punished with seven days arrest due to careless maneuvering which endangered the life of his observer and caused the destruction of a valuable aircraft. Only the mitigating circumstance of previous good conduct in the field has prevented more serious punishment."

"May this be warning to all of you," he added with stentorian voice, and to me: "Dismissed!"

I return my bedding to the supply room. Then a corporal, with carbine shouldered, comes to march me off. The way to the stockade leads through the middle of town. We walk on the street, I in front, the corporal behind me. I am staring down at the pavement. From the shoes of the passers-by, I notice that many stop to stare at us. The stockade is an old fortress, dark and bleak. The warder, a full-bearded old codger, accompanies his work with encouraging prattle:

"So you can't hang yourself," he says as he takes my suspenders.

"So you can't stab yourself," as I hand over my pocket knife.

"And now the teeth."

"Why teeth?" I ask.

"So you won't bite your throat while you sleep," he says. Everybody laughs, except me; I don't feel like it.

Then I'm locked into my cell. It is a small, bare room with a wooden cot, a stool, and a wash basin, nothing else. Outside the window is a steel loading chute, open toward the top. A small patch of sky was visible, as though one were looking up from the bottom of a deep cistern.

The key turns, and I'm alone. Alone with my thoughts. How long, I don't know. Then, steps reverberate from the stone tile, the door is swung open: the rounds!

I jump to attention.

The commander, an elderly warrant officer, says: "Say after me: Pfc. Udet . . ." his voice sounds mighty in the bare room.

"Pfc. Udet . . ." I repeat. And word for word booms on for me to echo:

". . . serves seven days . . . arrest . . . because he . . .

through careless maneuvering . . . endangered the life . . . of his observer . . . and destroyed a valuable aircraft."

The procession marches off. But in the evening it returns. And again, the commander begins: "Pfc. Udet . . . serves . . ."

By the next day I know the little speech by heart and recite it without prompting. During my arrest I must do this twice daily, fourteen times in all.

The first noon meal I leave sitting there. Barley without anything, "blue Heinrich" in the prison jargon. The red-bearded warden, quite unconcerned, takes the metal pot back with him.

"Appetite comes with doing time," he comments dryly as he walks out. In the evening he throws a mattress into my cell. It's filled with heather. The sky in the window square darkens, and I lie down. There, a bite in the thigh, another in the left shoulder . . . bed bugs!

It's a long night. Once I sleep on the bare cot, another time on the mattress on the floor, finally on the bare stone floor. The bed bugs are bad, but the thoughts are worse. The iron window hatches stand like great pointed ears on the prison walls. They serve as baffles that amplify all noises from above into the cells. The airfield is close by, and from early morning I hear the sputtering of the starting engines, then the low organ drone when the prop whips the air.

But I will never again hold a stick in my hands. Never again will I see the world disappear beneath me in a blue haze. What did I do? Turned a curve. Surely, curving is forbidden. Only a month ago they put Rieger in front of a court-martial and sentenced him to a year in prison. Because he curved over the airfield. "Disobedience in front of the troops," decided the court. I got off easy. But is this restriction not paper nonsense, doped out behind a desk by people who never sat behind a stick? Did not my crash prove those who made this regulation right? Questions, questions, and no answers. I think of my parents. My father never let on, but I know how proud he is that I am a pilot. And now they are going to pack me off as unsuitable! But, what is worse, I shouldn't be able to fly any more.

The seven days pass as though they were seven years. On the last day, redbeard brings me coffee. I shake my head; I don't want to drink.

"It's included with the lodgings," he invites.

But I have to return to my unit; I must find out what is going to happen to me. I'll probably have to report to the sergeant major's office: "Pfc. Udet, who has done seven days because he . . ." It will probably rattle after me like a chain. But it is to be different.

At the base everyone is running back and forth. No one pays any attention to me. During the morning, a bombing raid on Belfort has been ordered, with all available machines. The last have just taken off, and everyone is excited and pre-occupied with the extent of the affair.

"Hey, you—private!" someone shouts behind me. I turn around. It's a lieutenant. I don't know him. He must have arrived during the last few days.

"Are you a pilot?" he asks breathlessly.

Hope springs up in me: "Yes sir!"

"Well, man"—he shakes his head in surprise, touched with reproach—then: "Let's go, on the double, so we won't miss the show."

We run together toward the hangars. There, an old AVG is being tanked up. The lieutenant, sparking with zeal, rousts the mechanics. The bird is pulled from the cage, readied for takeoff, and small bombs are stowed in the observer's cockpit. We climb in.

"Ready?"

"Ready!"

"Go!"

A few hops over the grass, then the machine lifts off slowly. We are flying.

It is quite an old plucked crow. Probably a retired training machine. But never before did I experience the wonder of flying quite so deeply and strongly as in those moments. Below us the mountains, cut by ravines, their lean flanks covered with dark pine forests or the colorful shabracks of the fall leaves. It is a warm day, late in the fall. The wind sings softly in the braces, and before us the white clouds silently grow into the sky.

The enemy had already been aroused by the attack of the others. Two Farmans and a Morane monoplane approach from the direction of Belfort. It would be useless to fight. We have no machine gun on board, and our old bird claws along with effort at eighteen hundred meters.

The observer turns around and points to the south. We turn off. It is noon by now, and we fly straight into the sun.

Above Montreux, my "Franz" becomes fidgety. Below are depots and barracks, the last opportunity to place our bombs with advantage. Like a bird of prey, I make wide turns over the city. My observer seems to have his own technique for throwing bombs. Instead of throwing them overboard, he opens a small hatch below his seat and lets them fall straight down. His success proves him right. Looking over the side, I observe roof tile flying in all directions. A cloud rises to the sky.

Suddenly, he turns around and, looking horrified, points down. Slowly I understand. A bomb has slipped away from him and become stuck in the undercarriage. A slight shock is quite sufficient to set it off. Its charge is quite adequate to take care of us and the machine.

Carefully, I bank the plane to the left. "Wild maneuvering is forbidden!" How I wish that the C.O. was here at the wheel! The bomb follows the motions of the plane, slides to the left, and lies there. I curve to the right. The bomb now glides to the right, as though it were running on a curtain rod.

The observer disappears from his seat. He is kneeling in the bottom of his cockpit and, with a leg thrust through the hatch, frantically angles for the axle. But his leg is too short; he can't reach the bomb.

As a last resort, I go into a steep bank, the first of my life. The old crate responds sluggishly. We are almost perpendicular.

A slight clicking, and the bomb is loose and falls away. I straighten the aircraft and look after it, observing its impact in an open field. A fountain of earth shoots up.

We turn and head for home. My "Franz" is still waving his leg around in the air. He makes an exasperated gesture. His leg is stuck in the narrow hatch, and he cannot get it loose until after we have landed. In front of a blue ridge, the star-shaped fortifications of Neubreisach appear, our airfield.

The mechanics come running, along with some flight trainees. We are the last to return from the flight to Belfort. We climb out, and the observer shakes my hand. "I'm pleased to have made your acquaintance," he says.

An ordnance man comes running across the field toward us. I'm to report to the C.O.'s office at once.

There sits the captain. The same who had polished me off in front of the formation. I click my heels together and report: "Pfc. Udet returned from arrest."

He looks at me for a long while. Then, he says: "You are transferred to the Single-Seater Combat Command at Habsheim. Your aircraft will arrive in two days, then you can take off!"

He reaches for a file and leafs through it, as though I weren't there. I stand there for a while, motionless, surprised, and shaken. The captain looks up: "Dismissed!" I walk out. The airfield lies in the afternoon sun. It is the lunchtime rest period. All is quiet and peaceful, as on a Sunday. I stand there and take a few deep breaths.

Single-seater pilot? Fighter pilot? That of which all of us dream? I don't get it, I simply don't get it . . . .

The office orderly comes by with a couple of pots of coffee. "Well, sir fighter pilot," he grins and puts down one of the pots.

Company clerks are all-knowing, and when they smoke, they become talkative. I hold an open cigarette box toward him. He understands at once. With a sly, sidelong glance he takes three, lights one of them with much ado, and begins. This morning, the air staff officer from Muelhausen had called, wanting to know if Pfc. Udet had returned from arrest. Everyone had looked for me until the mechanics reported that I had taken off for the bombing raid on Belfort with Lieutenant Hartmann. This had been reported to Muelhausen. "Directly from arrest?" the air staff officer had asked. "Directly from arrest!" the captain had answered. Then Muelhausen rang off. Two hours later, the orders arrived: *Pfc. Udet is transferred to the Single-Seater Combat Command Habsheim.* "More luck than brains," mumbled the captain as he put the receiver down.

The orderly picked up the coffee mugs. "Well, then, good luck, *Herr Jagdflieger!*"‡ he says and trots off.

‡ "Mr. Fighter Pilot."

When the sun climbs high, the valleys warm up. The flight trainees, who had regarded me as an outcast, are now gathering. "Single-seater pilot at Habsheim? Son of a gun!" They want to know where I got my Iron Cross. I give them the information, somewhat loftily.

Two days later my machine arrives. A spanking new Fokker. It looks graceful and racy as a hawk. Beside it, the old Aviatik I flew at 206 seemed plump as a goose.

Half the flight students assembled for my takeoff. "Always practice diligently, boys," I shout as I wave at them. The chocks are yanked out from under the wheels, the Gnome snarls, and I'm off. The machine turns to the right. I am barely a meter off the ground. I jerk the stick to the left, leaning against it with all my might. Nothing happens, absolutely nothing. The hangar comes at me with blinding speed. A crash, splinters fly about me . . . I've crashed into the hangar!

For a while I sit motionless, as if paralyzed by the shock. Then I rise on shaky knees and climb out of the cockpit. I am safe and sound, but the aircraft is a shambles.

The students and mechanics come running across the field. All have seen my accident. Even from the barracks and the office they come running. They stand around me in a large semicircle, curiously eying the machine. A few come at me with questions I can't answer. I stand mute, everything inside me shaking. The captain arrives and looks at me. "So," he says as though he had expected this to happen. I stammer something: "Stick blocked, wings couldn't be warped."

"We'll investigate that," he says, and nods at the senior mechanic.

I go to my room and sit by the window, looking out with unseeing eyes, oblivious to all that is going on. The others, commiserating with me, leave me alone.

In the evening, the result of the investigation becomes known. The Bowden gear of the machine gun got tangled with the toggle board of the gas feed, thus blocking the steering. The senior mechanic has photographed the cockpit. I am exonerated. The pool furnishes me with another machine, but this time it's an old Fokker.

Next morning, I fly off to Habsheim. Only the mechanics are out on the airfield, no one else. It's a gray, foggy morning.

FIRST COMBATS

The Single-Seater Combat Command Habsheim consists of four pilots. Lieutenant Pfaelzer is the C.O., and besides me there are Sergeant Weingaertner and Corporal Glinkermann. We are all young people and live like princes in the vacant villa of a rich American who fled at the outset of the war.

A pleasant tone prevails among the men of the command. Weingaertner and I soon become friends. This is one of the things about Weingaertner. By the third day of acquaintance everyone befriends him.

Glinkermann is more difficult and remote. In the evening, he often sits with the mechanics, smoking his pipe and staring into the fog, which rises from the meadows in white clouds. I think he is quite poor and very much depressed about it. Much later, when his wallet is brought to me, I find a picture of a girl riding at the head of a laughing cavalcade. He had never spoken about it. Some jibe at him when he comes along with the wrappings of his leggings in perpetual disarray with a bit of white from his long johns showing through. But he is a good flier, one of the best I've known.

Duty is easy and comfortable. Once or twice a day we take off to fly cover for about an hour. But we hardly ever see the enemy. The December sky is cold and clear, the earth brittle with frost. If one wraps up well and butters the face, flying is a pleasure. Almost like a sleigh ride on the clouds.

Up in Flanders and in Champagne, where there is fighting and pilots are falling daily on both sides, they speak of the sleeping armies in the Vosges. It is said a little disparagingly, touched with envy.

One morning the alarm sounds quite early. This is unusual.

The forward observers report that a Caudron has passed over the lines and is heading in our direction. I climb into my crate and take off. The clouds hang low, a ceiling of barely four hundred meters. I push into the gray haze and climb higher and higher.

At two thousand meters a blue sky arches above me, with a strangely pale December sun shining down. I look around. Far back in the west, above the carpet of the clouds, I see a small dot, like a ship cruising on the horizon of the sea— the Caudron. I head straight for him, and he continues to come toward me. We close quickly. I can already recognize the wide wing span, the two motors, and the gondola hanging, narrow like the body of a bird of prey, between the wings. We are at the same altitude, going toward each other. This is against all the rules, because the Caudron is an observation plane, but I am a fighter. Pressing the button on my stick would send a stream of bullets belching from my machine gun, sufficient to tear him up in the air. He must know this as well as I. Just the same, he continues straight toward me.

He is now so close, I can make out the head of the observer. With his square goggles he looks like a giant, malevolent insect coming toward me to kill. The moment has come when I must fire. But I can't. It is as though horror has frozen the blood in my veins, paralyzed my arms, and torn all thought from my brain with the swipe of a paw. I sit there, flying on, and continue to stare, as though mesmerized, at the Caudron now to my left. Then the machine gun barks across to me. The impacts on my Fokker sound like metallic clicks. A tremor runs through my machine, a solid whack on my cheek, and my goggles are torn off. I reach up instinctively. Fragments, glass splinters from my goggles. My hand is wet with blood.

I push the stick, nose down, and dive into the clouds. I'm benumbed. How did this happen, how was it possible?

"You were timid, you were a coward," hammers the motor. And then, only one thought: "Thank God, no one saw this!"

The flowing green, the pine tops, the airfield. I land. The mechanics come running. I don't wait for them. I climb out of the cockpit and head for the quarters. The medic removes the glass splinters with a pair of tweezers. They had bored into the flesh around my eyes. It should hurt, but I don't feel a thing.

Then I go up to my room and throw myself onto my bed. I want to sleep, but my thoughts return over and over, allowing no relaxation. Is it cowardice when one fails in the first moment of combat? I want to calm myself and say: "Nerves —it can happen to anyone. Next time you'll do better!" But my conscience refuses to be satisfied with such an easy declaration. It presents me with the hard fact: You failed, because in the moment of combat you thought of yourself, you were afraid for your life. At this moment I recognize the meaning of soldiering.

To be a soldier means to think of the enemy and of victory and to forget one's self in the process! It is possible that the line of demarcation between the man and the coward is narrow as the edge of a sword. But he who would remain a man among men must, at the moment of decision, have the strength to choke off the animal fear within himself, because the animal within ourselves wants to live at any price. And he who gives in to it will forever be lost to the fraternity of men where honor, duty, and belief in the Fatherland is the credo.

I step to the window and look down. Weingaertner and Glinkermann are walking up and down in front of the house. Perhaps they never had to face up to it as I just did, and I promise myself that from this moment on I will be nothing but a soldier. I will shoot straighter and fly better than my comrades until I have wiped out the blot against my honor.

Together with Behrend, who has followed me to Habsheim, I go to work. We make a silhouette model of a Nieuport, as it would be seen from behind during an attack. Evenings, when flying activities have come to an end, I set up the target in the middle of the airfield. From three hundred meters I dive down, and at one hundred meters I open fire. I pull out at a very low altitude and climb again, and the game begins anew. Behrend has to count the hits, and he signals to me. Hits in the motor count double, and ten hits mean a glass of beer for him. Often I have stoppages—too often. Behrend and I often work late into the night to eliminate these malfunctions.

Then the results improve. Actually, they improve surprisingly fast. I'm quite happy until I discover that Behrend helps with the pencil. Out of friendship for me, he claims, but I think it's for his love of beer.

Orders come down that ammunition is to be conserved, so I have to cut down on my practice flights. By way of compensation, however, we now frequently attack the French trenches from the air.

One evening, on one of these trench flights, I am a bit behind schedule. It is up north, close to Thaun. The enemy machine gun nests, bedded and hidden in pine forests, have proved tempting targets. By the time I fly back to the airstrip, night has fallen.

Below, they light pitch torches to guide me home. Their reddish glow flickers across the field, giving a diffuse and restless illumination. I line up for the landing. It is difficult to see the ground. I touch down hard enough to damage the undercarriage. Otherwise the machine is fine, but I will be out of action for a day at least.

I tell Behrend and the other mechanic I want them out on

the field at four-thirty the next morning. Behrend pulls a face. The next day is a Sunday, and when Behrend is expected to work on Sundays he suddenly becomes religious.

The lead gray of the morning light lies on the airfield as we begin our work. The woods stand about us like a darkly threatening phalanx. The bare wooden walls of the small hangars reflect a pale light. A peculiar mood prevails, as though something extraordinary were in the air. I'm not sure whether it will mean good or bad luck.

At six, the church bells in the surrounding towns begin to chime, and their sound drifts over to us across the treetops. The sun has risen, and we continue to work silently. It has gotten so warm, we sweat even though we are wearing only our blue work jackets. At twelve noon we finish. Behrend and his buddy make a fast getaway; they still want to catch the train to Muelhausen.

It is quiet now, everyone has gone to town on pass. I drive to our quarters and eat lunch. I have the table all to myself and have the coffee brought to me out in the garden. There, I sit in a field chair smoking and stare into the sky.

At three-thirty a telephone operator comes running with a report from the observers in the forward trenches: Two French aircraft have passed over the lines and are rapidly approaching Altkirch.

I jump into the car and go tearing off to the airfield. Without thinking, instinct tells me with certainty: This is it! The machine is ready to start, and mechanics are standing around. The telephone operator had had enough presence of mind to rouse everyone still on the base. I climb into the cockpit and take off.

I claw my way up in the direction of the front lines. I must try to gain superior height so I might have the edge in the flight. Twenty-eight hundred meters . . . I fly west toward

Altkirch. Just as I am above Altkirch, I see them. I count: One . . . two . . . three . . . four . . . I reach up to wipe my goggles . . . this is impossible, it can't be! Those black dots must be oil flecks, spray from the motor. But no, the dots remain, and they grow larger. Seven, I count, seven in a row, and beyond them another wave appears, again five and again . . . they are coming closer, sharply silhouetted against the yellow silken flush of the afternoon sky. Twenty-two of them, bombers of the Caudron and Farman types. They come buzzing on like a swarm of angry hornets, pell-mell, without any discernible formation. High above the others glides the queen of the swarm, a mighty Voisin. I pull at the stick. We are closing fast. They certainly must have taken notice of me, but they act as though I don't exist. They don't climb a single centimeter and hold steadily to their course, east-northeast toward Muelhausen. I look around. The blue shell of the sky behind me is empty. None of my buddies from Habsheim have taken off. I am alone.

I reach them near Burnhaupt. Three hundred meters above them I make a wide turn and fall in with them on the course toward Muelhausen. I lean overboard to look at the gaggle of twenty-three machines, in the center a giant Farman. Between their wings I see bits of the ground, blue slate roofs, red tile. This is it! My heart is beating in my throat. My hands, grabbing the stick, are damp. One against twenty-three!

My Fokker flits above the gaggle like a hound chasing the boar. He pursues him—but he doesn't attack. At this moment I know: If this second passes without a fight, then it's good-bye fighter piloting for me. I will have no recourse but to request a transfer away from the command.

We are over Dornbach, closely before Muelhausen. In the coffee gardens of the inns are people, colored flecks in the green-brown of the landscape. They are running back and forth, gesticulating and pointing up.

Then I clear the hurdle. From this instant on I see only one thing: That big Farman in the middle of the formation. I nose down, gather speed, and dive at full throttle. The enemy aircraft grows in front of me, becoming larger as though he were being hastily focused in a microscope. The observer stands up. I can see his round leather helmet. He whips up his machine gun and points it at me.

At eighty meters I want to fire, but I must be absolutely certain. Closer, closer, forty meters, thirty, now! Whatever the barrel will spit out . . . tack . . . tack . . . tack. There, he totters. A blue flame shoots from his exhaust, he lists, and white smoke belches forth—hit, hit in the gas tank!

Clack . . . clack . . . clack—with metallic sounds bullets hit my machine just in front of the cockpit. I whip my head around and look to the rear. Two Caudrons covering me with machine gun bursts. I remain calm. This will be done just as during the practice sessions at the airfield. Stick forward, and I dive down. Three hundred meters below I pull out.

The fuselage of the Farman dives down past me like a giant torch, trailing a black cloud from which bright flames spurt forth. A man, his arms and legs spread out like a frog's, falls past—the observer.

At the moment, I don't think of them as human beings. I feel only one thing: Victory, triumph, victory! The iron vise about my breast has burst, and the blood courses through my body in mighty, free spurts.

The air above me is now filled with the thundering organ of the motors. In between, the hasty barking of the machine guns. All available machines have now risen from Habsheim and thrown themselves upon the enemy. Under the violence of their impact, the French squadron has broken up, and a number of single combats have ensued. Wherever one looks, there are machines twisting about in dogfights.

A single Caudron is making a hasty exit to the west. He's not being followed. I chase after him at full throttle. The intoxication of the first fight has passed. The destruction of the enemy has become a tactical problem, nothing more.

I open fire at 150 meters and stop again. Too far, much too far. At eighty meters I let go with the second burst. This time I can clearly observe the effect. The Caudron trembles, the right engine puffs a small cloud of smoke, the prop slows up and stops. The pilot turns around and sees me. In a moment he goes down into a steep dive.

I stay with him. He's flying with only one engine; he can't get away from me. I am now so close to him I can feel his propwash.

A new burst—the pilot collapses on his stick. Then—stoppage! During the steep dive, the cartridges have loosened in the belt. I hammer at the gun with both fists. No good, it remains silent.

Out of action, I have no choice but to leave my opponent and return home. At five-twenty-five I land on the airfield at Habsheim. I had taken off at four-sixteen. The entire play has reeled off in an hour.

In the middle of the airstrip stands Captain Mackenthun, the C.O. of Habsheim Base. He stands straddle-legged, binoculars to the eyes, watching the fighting. I walk toward him: "Sergeant Udet returned from sortie. Farman two-seater brought down!" He takes the binoculars down and looks at me, his face emotionless, as though frozen in position. "Our large plane has just crashed over Napoleon's Island," he says.

I know that Lieutenant Kurth was the pilot and Mackenthun's best friend. I salute and walk toward the hangars.

Not until evening can we sort out the events of the day.

The French air attack, the first large-scale air attack ever on Germany, has been beaten off. Five enemy machines have been brought down on our side of the lines. Of the nine officers of one unit, who had started at noon, only three return. *"Tu finiras aussi à l'Île Napoléon!"* has become the slogan when one wants to undertake a daring coup.

Three of our own men did not return: Kurth, Hopfgarten, and Wallat, the crew of the AEG G-type aircraft from the 48th Abteilung. They had attacked a Farman, were rammed during the dogfight, and the two went down in a ball of wreckage, just above Napoleon's Island. It happened on March 18, 1916.

In our villa in Habsheim, the windows remain lit up until late into the night. Men were killed on this day, but this time we were not merely along for the ride. Pfaelzer, Weingaertner, Glinkermann, and I each got his man.

We are young, and we celebrate our victory.

DEATH FLIES FASTER

At noon the order arrives: The entire *staffel* [squadron] will move! In the evening we are already packed and waiting at the railroad station in Muelhausen. The platform is full of people. We look ghostly in the pale light of the lamps, which are shaded against aerial observation. Many women are in the crowd, and most of them are crying. For two years we were quartered just outside Muelhausen, where we spent all of our free time. We had formed many attachments and had become part of the town, as though we were natives.

I share a compartment with Esser. His fiancée has come over from Freiburg to see him off. A lovely girl with a proud, inscrutable face. She doesn't cry. They are leaning out of the car window, talking. "Remember to wear your gloves and underclothes," she says. The corners of her mouth quiver as she talks. One can feel that she really wants to speak of other things.

Then the train rolls off into the night, destination unknown. We feel that the quiet days have come to an end and that we will be thrown in at some hot spot up front. This feeling fills us with tension, mixed with just a little bit of apprehension. Will we be able to meet the challenges of the great battle of the air?

For three days and three nights we are shunted back and forth behind the lines, as though we were in a giant switch yard. Ammunition trains roll by, and hospital trains with their cargo of misery invisible behind windows painted white. At nightfall of the third day we are unloaded. We look around and then at each other. "Lause-Champagne," mumbles our leader.

A thin, cold rain is falling, wrapping the flatlands into a gray mantle of desolation. A few shapely poplars along the highway freeze in the March wind. We are quartered in the small town of La Selve. Esser and I stay together. Our room is depressingly austere, but Esser soon comes up with a solution. He and his orderly commandeer red velvet curtains from a deserted estate. A pair of red silk pajamas are transformed into a lamp shade. Thus our room takes on an air of sultry comfort.

Across from us, the élite of the French air service is deployed. Even Nungesser is supposed to be among them—and Guynemer, ace of aces and the Richthofen of the enemy. They fly the single-seat Spad with the 180-horsepower Hispano. A fast, agile machine, superior to our Shark and Albatros, especially in the dive, when our wing planes begin to quake so that we fear they'll tear off in the air. The more sturdy Spad takes these stresses much better. The ground defenses are much better organized than in the Vosges. I notice that on my very first flight. A flak fragment shatters the head brace, and I have difficulty bringing the aircraft back home.

Nearly all dogfights are inconclusive, and our morale sinks lower each day. One evening, Esser and I sit in our room. His resourceful orderly has turned up a Gramophone. We stuff a wad of cloth into its horn to dampen it, and now it sounds as melancholy as the song of a country girl in the backyard of a tenement. Esser sits there and writes to his fiancée, as he does every day, making plans for the future.

On April 16, our *staffel* finally has its first success. Glinkermann brings down a Caudron, Esser a Nieuport. The others observe Esser pursuing another enemy aircraft until he disappears in the west. We hear nothing further, and I spend the night alone in the room with the red velvet curtains.

On the next day we receive a call from the trenches. Our

C.O. drives there, and toward evening he returns. In the car is a bag so small, as though it were only holding a child, all that is left of Esser.

The C.O. writes to his parents; I am supposed to write to his fiancée in Freiburg. It is a difficult letter, the most difficult I have ever written—but I will have to write many more of these.

On the morning after Esser's funeral, Puz approaches me. His round, snub-nosed face is full of sympathy.

"You know, Knaegges," he says, "it must be terrible, all alone in that room, with the empty bed. If you want, I'll move in with you."

We shake hands, and in the evening the orderly takes the small white calling card off the door. "Lieutenant Haenisch" it says now, where it used to say "Lieutenant Esser."

On April 24, I achieve my first victory on this front. Above Chavignon I meet a Nieuport and flame him after a short flight. I see him burst to pieces among the shell holes. It is my fifth confirmed victory, because after my first fight above Muelhausen I brought down three more while based at Habsheim.

My birthday comes two days later, on the twenty-sixth. I have invited all my buddies to the red salon. Three pound cakes have been baked with Behrend's help. We also have cocoa and the table, decked out in white, stands in the middle of the room, just as it would be for a children's party.

We sit around shooting the breeze as we await the return of our C.O., First Lieutenant Reinhold. Two hours ago he had started out on a patrol, together with two others. At two o'clock the other two return. They say they had lost sight of him during a dogfight, when he pursued a fleeing opponent into the clouds. They are embarrassed. Certainly, their tale could be true. But there remains the shadow of doubt, because, in the air, a formation belongs together like arm and hand, like head and body. Each is responsible for the life of the man ahead of him as though it were his own. This is done so that the man ahead of him, at the head of the wedge, has his back free and can concentrate on the attack.

At three-thirty I say, "Let's go to it. If he's late, he'll have to eat by himself."

They start packing it in. Although they are all hungry and the cake tastes great, they leave two pieces of each. Reinhold is somehow among us. No one speaks of him, but our thoughts keep returning to him. It is discernible in the conversation, which is flagging and aimless, dying down almost as soon as it gets under way.

At five, the telephone rings. Glinkermann, sitting closest, takes the receiver and winks at me as he hands it to me. But the others have noticed, and dead silence descends upon the room. At the other end of the line, a bored voice: "Are you missing a pilot?"

"Yes sir," I say hastily.

Silence on the other end. Then, a whispered exchange— here and there I catch a word—"What did he look like, you dummox?" . . . The bored voice comes back: "Did your pilot wear something other than a flying cap?"

I remember that Reinhold always wore his garrison cap with a pair of earmuffs over it.

"Yes," I shout, "is Lieutenant Reinhold there?"

"We found no papers," and quietly: "What was the regimental number, Otto?" Then, louder, to me: "It said "135" on the shoulder straps."

"Dead?"

"Yes!"

"Where are you, we'll come at once."

"Near Lierval. You can see the aircraft from a long way off." I hang up and look at the others. All are pale and serious. "Let's go!" I say. We run to the car and race along the shell-marked highway toward Lierval.

Reinhold's machine lies in the middle of an open field. It is almost undamaged. It looks as though it could take off again any second. We run across the green seedlings toward the aircraft. The infantrymen report: Reinhold sat behind the stick, right hand on the machine gun button. His face was frozen in the tension of his last combat, the left eye squinting, the right wide open, as though he were still aiming at an invisible enemy. Thus, death overtook him. A bullet had penetrated his head from behind, coming out in front between the eyebrows. The entry and exit holes are quite small. We pick up the dead man and take him with us. "This is the way I would like to die," says Glinkermann to me.

A few days later, our new C.O. arrives—Lieutenant Gontermann. A great reputation precedes him. He has brought down twelve aircraft and six balloons and is regarded as the flying service's leading specialist for "captive hogs."

His tactics are entirely new and surprising to us. Before he opens fire, he defeats his enemy by outflying him. When he finally fires, he requires, at most, a dozen rounds to tear apart the other's machine, because, by that time, he has usually closed in to about twenty meters, flying in his opponent's propwash.

He exudes great calm. His broad farmer's face rarely exhibits the least bit of emotion. He is a profound believer. But one thing about him gets me: He is irritated by every hit he finds in his machine after he lands. In this he sees proof of his shortcomings as a flier. With his system, a

properly conducted dogfight does not permit his opponent
to get a single well-placed round off. In this respect he is
entirely different from Richthofen. The Red Baron acknowl-
edges his mechanics' reports of hits in his crate with a smile
and a shrug.

Almost simultaneously with Gontermann's arrival, the
staffel is moved from La Selve back to Boncourt. It is an
old French castle in the middle of a park with large, rangy
rooms. The owner, an elderly provincial noble, lives there with
his wife and two daughters. They have withdrawn to the
more remote section of the house and given the luxurious
rooms over to us. They probably hate us, but their behavior
is quite correct. If we meet one of them in the hallways
or in the park, they greet us with icy courtesy.

One day, all this changes. At the noon table, Gontermann
tells us that he has met the master of the house in the corridor.
The old man was crying. His daughters have to go down into
the village to work in the fields. The town commandant, a
private first class, badgers and annoys them whenever he
can. Apparently he is trying to make out with the younger
one, a lean, half-grown sparrow of fifteen. Gontermann prom-
ises to look into the matter. His face is red with anger as
he relates this to us.

In the afternoon, the private comes trotting up, mounted
high on a fat mare. We have set our coffee table under the
trees in the garden. The windows of Gontermann's room
are open, and we can hear every word.

"A complaint has been made about you," begins Gontermann. He speaks quietly but louder than usual. "You are
said to work the women too long and too hard."

"That is my privilege, *Herr Leutnant!*" The tone of the
private is confident and challenging.

"How so?"

"When these broads are fresh and disobedient, they have to be punished!"

Gontermann's voice becomes louder: "You are also said to have made unseemly advances to some of the women."

A long pause, then again Gontermann's voice: "For example, the little *comtesse* here at the castle."

"I am not responsible to you in these matters, *Herr Leutnant;* I'm the town commandant here!"

Gontermann's bellow comes back so loud, we all jump.

"You are what? You are a filthy swine! An animal! A character who should be put up against the wall without further ado! We fight with honest weapons against an honest enemy, and a knave like you comes along and mucks up the works!"

It's like a medieval execution. For an uninterrupted five minutes Gontermann smote him, smote him with words. But this did not soften the punishment.

"I am going to place you before a court-martial," he shouts in the end: *"Raus!"*

The private walks past us. His face is pale and covered with perspiration. In his agitation, he forgets to salute, and he also leaves his horse behind. Then comes Gontermann. He has already calmed down.

We take off for an evening patrol. Gontermann brings down a Nieuport, I a Spad. It's my sixth victory.

Next morning, Behrend, who lives in the village with the other mechanics, tells me that the town commander has been marched off by the field gendarmes. Gontermann's influence is considerable. Much more so than his rank would indicate. Upstairs they know what they have in him. During the two weeks he has been with the *staffel,* he has brought down eight opponents. Then comes his *Pour le Mérite** and four weeks' leave. On the eve of his departure he hands command of the *staffel* over to me until his return.

We fly every day, whenever the weather permits, in any way at all. Mostly three times: morning, noon, and evenings. Our sorties are almost always cover missions, and real fights rarely take place. The French work very cautiously in the air, but tactically they are excellent performers. We all have the feeling that the enemy is superior in this field, and not merely due to better aircraft. Twenty months' experience on a major battle front and the toughening occasioned by hundreds of combats make for a lead that is not easily overcome.

On May 25 we fly cover—in wedge formation as usual. I lead, behind me the Wendel brothers, then Puz and Glinkermann. We are at about two thousand meters altitude. The sky is clear, as though it had been swept. Way up above, there are a few feather clouds. The sun beats down on us. It's about noon, and no sight of the enemy far and wide. From time to time I turn around and nod at the others. They fly behind me, the Wendel brothers, Puz, and Glinkermann—everything as it should be.

I don't know if there is such a thing as a sixth sense. But suddenly I'm certain we are in some sort of danger. I make a half turn—and in that instant I see, close to my side, not twenty meters off, Puz's aircraft enveloped in fire and smoke. But Puz himself sits straight up in the center of this inferno, head turned toward me. Now he slowly lifts his right arm to his crash helmet. It could be the last convulsion, but it looks as though he were saluting me—for the last time.

---

* The highest German award for valor. It was given the nickname "The Blue Max" by some English officers.

"Puz," I scream, "Puz!"

Then his machine breaks up. The fuselage dives straight down like a fiery meteor, the broken wing planes trundling after it. I am stunned as I stare over the side after the wreckage. An aircraft moves into the range of my sight and tears westward about five hundred meters below me. The cockades blink up at me like malicious eyes. At the same moment I have the feeling that it can only be Guynemer!

I push down, I have to get him! But the wings of the Albatros are not up to the strain. They begin to flutter more and more, so that I fear the machine will disintegrate in the air. I give up the pursuit and return home. The others have already landed.

They are standing in a group on the airstrip, talking in low and dejected tones. Glinkermann stands apart from the rest. He is lost in thought, scratching designs into the ground with his cane. His dog, standing at his side, nuzzles him at the knee. His mind, however, is so far off he ignores the animal completely.

As I approach, he lifts his head and looks at me: "You mustn't be mad at me, Knaegges, but I really couldn't prevent it. He came at us out of the sun, and by the time I knew what was going on, it was all over."

His face looks pained. I know him well enough to realize that he will torture himself for weeks with self-recrimination, because he flew behind Puz and because he should have prevented it.

But I also know what sort of comrade Glinkerle is. When I fly with him I feel safe, because he would rather be shot to pieces than expose my back even for a moment.

"Leave it be, Glinkerle," I say to him and pat him on the back, "no one was at fault, or we are all equally responsible."

Then I go to my quarters and write my report, first for "upstairs," then the letter for Haenisch's parents.

Death flies faster . . .

An orderly rouses me out of my noonday nap. A call from Mortiers: An aircraft of our *staffel* has crashed there. The pilot, Sergeant Mueller, is dead.

I drive over. A few old soldiers, gray and weathered like the clay of Champagne, are waiting for me. They have laid him out in a barn and lead me to him. His face is quiet and peaceful. He probably had a quick and easy death. I listen to an account of the accident and return to Boncourt.

It is quiet on the airfield. In the afternoon all had taken off. Toward evening they return by twos and threes. Glinkermann is not with them. The two who flew with him had lost sight of him. He disappeared in the clouds flying west. The same old tune, the same bitter tune . . .

On the airfield, rammed into the ground, stands a cane. A cap is draped over it. Glinkermann's charm. When he takes off, he leaves them there; when he returns he takes them back. A large wolf-gray shepherd uneasily cruises about the cane. As I walk across the airfield, he trots after me. Normally, he never does this. He is devoted only to Glinkermann and snaps at anyone coming too close to him. His damp, cold muzzle affectionately pushes into my hand.

It is difficult for me to maintain my composure. But Gontermann has left me in command, and no one shall see me weaken. I want the orderly room to phone all units we can reach to inquire if a flier had landed up front.

"All?" asks the clerk.

"All, of course, all!" I shout at the man.

"As soon as you come up with anything, let me know

at once; I'll be in my room." I have gotten hold of myself and say it as quietly and coolly as I can.

The night comes slowly. I sit at the open window and look into the descending darkness. The narrow, silver sickle of the moon climbs slowly over the massive treetops of the park. The crickets are unbearably loud and shrill. It is quite humid, and it will probably rain during the night. Glinkermann's dog is in the room with me. He is restless, walking to the door and back again. Sometimes he gives a low whimper. Glinkermann, Glinkerle! Eight days ago he had brought down a Spad sitting on my neck, and the following day I crowded off an opponent pursuing him. He has to come back; he can't leave me alone.

At ten o'clock an orderly comes rushing into the room: "*Herr Leutnant,* come to the phone right away, an infantry post near Ogruevalles!"

A deep, dark voice. Yes, a German aircraft had come down near them. The pilot had black hair, parted in the middle. There were no other identifying marks. Everything had burned up. The dog howled so loudly, I had to get him out of the room. I light my desk lamp and have Glinkermann's orderly bring me his things. A worn wallet with some money in it, the picture of a girl, and part of a letter. "You dear!" it begins, but it was never completed.

Next morning, a rack wagon pulls into the yard. It carries a wooden box. It is unloaded and placed in Glinkerle's tent. We place his cap and oaken cane onto the box and cover its bare wood with flowers and green boughs.

Two days later we inter Glinkermann. On the morning of his last day, his promotion to the rank of lieutenant arrives. It would have made him very happy, if he had only lived to receive it. I have the warrant taken home to his parents by a man going on leave to Muelhausen. He also takes the dog along. The animal braces its paws against the ground and must be forcibly dragged from Glinkermann's tent. When the car rattles off, it still wails like a human being.

On June 4, Sergeant Eichenauer is killed in action. On this day I write to Grashoff, an old buddy from the days at Habsheim: "I want to go to another front, I would like to come to you. I'm the last of Jasta 15, the last of those who once left from Muelhausen to go to Champagne."

Jasta 15, which grew out of the old Single-Seater Combat Command Habsheim, has now only four aircraft, three sergeants, and myself as their leader. Almost always we fly alone. Only in this way can we fulfill our assigned duties.

Much is happening on the front. It is said the other side is preparing an offensive. The balloons are up every day, hanging in long rows in the summer sky, like a garland of fat-bellied clouds. It would be good if one of them were to burst. It would be a good warning to the others in addition, on just plain general principles.

I start early in the morning, so that I can have the sun at my back to stab down at the balloon. I fly higher than ever before. The altimeter shows five thousand meters. The air is thin and icy. The world below me looks like a gigantic aquarium. Above Lierval, where Reinhold fell, an enemy pusher type is cruising around. Like a tiny water flea, he shovels his way through the air.

From the west, a small dot approaches fast. At first, small and black, it grows quickly as it approaches. A Spad, an enemy fighter. A loner like me, up here, looking for prey. I settle myself into my seat. There's going to be a fight.

At the same height, we go for each other, passing at a hair's breadth. We bank into a left turn. The other's aircraft shines light brown in the sun. Then begins the circling. From below, it might appear as though two large birds of prey were courting one another. But up here it's a game of death. He who gets the enemy at his back first is lost, because the single-seater with his fixed machine guns can only shoot straight ahead. His back is defenseless.

Sometimes we pass so closely I can clearly recognize a narrow, pale face under the leather helmet. On the fuselage, between the wings, there is a word in black letters. As he passes me for the fifth time, so close that his propwash shakes me back and forth, I can make it out: *"Vieux"* it says there—*vieux*—the old one. That's Guynemer's sign.†

Yes, only one man flies like this on our front. Guynemer, who has brought down thirty Germans. Guynemer, who always hunts alone, like all dangerous predators, who swoops out of the sun, downs his opponents in seconds, and disappears. Thus he got Puz away from me. I know it will be a fight where life and death hang in the balance.

I do a half loop in order to come down on him from above. He understands at once and also starts a loop. I try a turn, and Guynemer follows me. Once out of the turn, he can get me into his sights for a moment. Metallic hail rattles through my right wing plane and rings out as it strikes the struts.

I try anything I can, tightest banks, turns, side slips, but with lightning speed he anticipates all my moves and reacts at once. Slowly I realize his superiority. His aircraft is better, he can do more than I, but I continue to fight. Another curve. For a moment he comes into my sights. I push the button on the stick . . . the machine gun remains silent . . . stoppage!

With my left hand clutched around the stick, my right

† The entire inscription on Guynemer's Spad read *"Vieux Charles"*—"Old Charlie."

attempts to pull a round through. No use—the stoppage can't be cleared. For a moment I think of diving away. But with such an opponent this would be useless. He would be on my neck at once and shoot me up.

We continue to twist and turn. Beautiful flying if the stakes weren't so high. I never had such a tactically agile opponent. For seconds, I forget that the man across from me is Guynemer, my enemy. It seems as though I were sparring with an older comrade over our own airfield. But this illusion lasts only for seconds.

For eight minutes we circle around each other. The longest eight minutes of my life. Now, lying on his back, he races over me. For a moment I have let go of the stick and hammer the receiver with both fists. A primitive expedient, but it helps sometimes.

Guynemer has observed this from above, he must have seen it, and now he knows what gives with me. He knows I'm helpless prey.

Again he skims over me, almost on his back. Then it happens: He sticks out his hand and waves to me, waves lightly, and dives to the west in the direction of his lines.

I fly home. I'm numb.

There are people who claim Guynemer had a stoppage himself then. Others claim he feared I might ram him in desperation. But I don't believe any of them. I still believe to this day that a bit of chivalry from the past has continued to survive. For this reason I lay this belated wreath on Guynemer's unknown grave.

On June 19, Gontermann returns from leave. His lips narrow when I tell him of the fate that has befallen the *staffel* during the past weeks. "Then two of us are all that is left, Udet," he says.

I have written to Grashoff, but at the moment I can't bring myself to raise the subject. I postpone the matter until evening.

During the afternoon, Gontermann has already flown his first sortie. He has brought down an opponent, and his own machine has taken twelve hits. I'm at the airfield when he lands, and we walk to the castle together.

For the first time I see him immediately following a fight. His face is pale and damp with perspiration. The rigid calm he always radiates is gone. I see before me a man whose nerves have been completely wrought up. This does not diminish him in my eyes; it only moves him closer to me. I admire this self-discipline, which enables him to keep a tight rein on himself at other times.

As we walk along together, he rails at himself in a low voice. The hits his aircraft took have upset him. I try to calm him.

"He who shoots must himself expect to be shot at," I say.

We walk over the grinding gravel of the park toward the house. A small white garden table stands there. He stops and scoops up a handful of gravel and a leaf. He puts the leaf on the table and lets the pebbles fall down on it slowly. Every time one of the pebbles hits the metal top of the table, the ring sounds like the impact of a bullet.

"You see, Udet, that's the way it is," he says while he is doing this, "the bullets fall from the hand of God"—he points at the leaf, "they come closer and closer. Sooner or later they will hit us. They will hit us for certain."

With a hasty motion of the hand, he sweeps the entire game from the table. I look at him sideways. He is wrought up deep down inside. I feel strange in his presence, and my desire to get away from him gets ever stronger. The very air of Boncourt lies heavily on my breast, pregnant with sad memories.

"I would like to transfer to Jasta 37," I say.

Gontermann whips around. "You want to leave me?" There is a strong note of reproach. But he gets hold of himself immediately, his face freezes, and he says in an icy voice: "It goes without saying that I won't place any difficulties in your way, Lieutenant Udet."

I can sense exactly what he thinks. "There are old buddies there, from Habsheim," I say in a low voice, "the last from the old Combat Command. Of course, I will help break in the replacements before I leave."

Gontermann is silent for a while. Then he holds out his hand: "It is really too bad that you won't stay with me, Udet, but I can see your point."

Three months later, Gontermann falls. Like many of our best, he fell through no fault of his own. His triplane lost a wing right over the airfield, and he crashed. Twenty-four hours later he died without regaining consciousness. It was a good death.

RICHTHOFEN

For the past six weeks I am the C.O. of Jasta 37. We are based in Wynghene, a small town in the middle of the Flanders marshes. The terrain is difficult, broken up by ground folds and water ditches. Here, every emergency landing means a crack-up. When one climbs high enough, one can see across to Ostende and the sea. Gray-green and endless, it stretches to the horizon.

Many were surprised at Grashoff leaving me in command when he was transferred to Macedonia. There are men here senior both in years and rank. But, back in the fall, when I brought down the three Englishmen over Lens, he had promised it to me. It was a surprise success in Guynemer's style. I came down out of the sun and attacked the last one on the outside left, finishing him with five rounds. Then the next one and, finally, the leader. The other two were so surprised, they didn't get a shot off. The whole thing didn't last more than twenty seconds, just as it was with Guynemer back then. In war, one must learn the trade of fighter piloting or get knocked off. There is no alternative.

When I landed, Grashoff knew all about it. "When I leave here some day, Knaegges, you will inherit the *staffel*," he said. Thus I became the C.O. of Jasta 37.

Across from us are the English. Young, sharp boys, they take on anybody and usually hold out until the final decision. But we are their equals. The depressing feeling of inferiority, giving us all the doldrums at Boncourt, has disappeared. The *staffel* has a long string of victories behind it, and I myself have, up to now, nineteen confirmed.

As the winter deepens, air traffic slows down. There is

much rain and snow. Even on dry days the heavy clouds drift so low that no takeoffs are ordered. We sit around in our rooms. I am quartered in the country house of a lace manufacturer. Sometimes, when I sit at the window, I see the home workers bringing up their wares. They are bent, ragged shapes, stamping through the snow.

The son of the house has entered the Royal Flying Corps* on the other side. But the people don't make me ill at ease over it. "He does his duty, I do mine," is their point of view, reasonable and clear.

In the spring of 1918 a restlessness runs along the German front, from Flanders up into the Vosges. This is certainly not the spring alone. Everywhere, among the officers and men, they are speaking of the great offensive, which is supposed to be imminent. But no one knows anything for certain. On March 15, the *staffel* is ordered to load up its personnel and aircraft at once. Destination unknown. We all know this is the beginning of the offensive.

Along the highway to Le Cateau we set up our aircraft tents. The rain comes down in a fine spray, which slowly turns everything—trees, houses, and people—into the same gray mush. I have put on my leather jacket and help the mechanics drive the tent pegs into the ground.

A car comes rattling along the road. Many cars pass this way, so we have ceased paying any attention to them. We continue to work in grim silence. Someone pats me on the back, and I jump around.

Richthofen. The rain is seeping down from his cap, running into his face.

"Hello, Udet," says the captain, and he tips his cap. "Nice rotten weather today."

I salute in silence and look at him. A quiet, self-controlled

* The Belgian Royal Flying Corps.

face, large, cold eyes, half covered by heavy lids. This is the man who has already brought down sixty-seven, the best of us all. His car stands on the highway below. He has clambered up the slope through the rain. I am waiting.

"How many have you brought down, Udet?"

"Nineteen confirmed, one pending," I answer.

His cane pokes around in the wet leaves.

"Hm, twenty then," he repeats. He looks up and gives me a searching glance.

"Then you would actually seem ripe for us. Would you like to?"

Would I like to? I most certainly would! If I had my way, I would pack up right now and go along with him. There are many good squadrons in the Army, and Jasta 37 is far from the worst. But there is only one Richthofen group.

"Yes, *Herr Rittmeister*," I reply, and we shake hands.

I look after him as his spare and slender shape clambers down the slope, climbs into the car, and disappears around the next bend behind a curtain of rain.

"Well, you could say we have made it now," says Behrend as I bend down beside him to continue driving the tent pegs into the ground.

There are many good squadrons on the front, but there is only one Richthofen group. And now I see the secret of their success unfold.

Other squadrons live in castles or small towns, twenty to thirty kilometers behind the front lines. The Richthofen group dwells in corrugated shacks that can be erected and broken down in a matter of hours. They are rarely more than twenty kilometers behind the foremost outposts. Other squadrons go up two or three times a day. Richthofen and his men fly five times a day. Others close down operations in bad weather; here they fly under almost any condition.

However, the biggest surprise for me is the forward combat airstrips. This was an invention of Boelcke, the senior master of the German air service. Richthofen, his most gifted pupil, has taken this practice over.

Just a few kilometers behind the lines, often within range of the enemy artillery, we are on fully dressed standby, lounging in reclining chairs in an open field. Our aircraft, gassed up and ready to go, are right alongside. As soon as an opponent appears on the horizon, we go up—one, two, or an entire *staffel*. Immediately after the fight we land, stretch out in our reclining chairs, and scour the sky with binoculars, waiting for the next opponent. Standing patrols are not flown. Richthofen doesn't believe in them. He'll allow only patrols into the enemy's rear areas. "This business of standing sentry duty in the air weakens the pilots' will to fight," he maintains. Thus we only go up to fight.

I arrive at the group at ten o'clock, and at twelve I'm already off on my first sortie with Jasta 11. In addition, Jastas 4, 6, and 10 make up the group.† Richthofen himself leads Jasta 11. He puts great store in personally trying out each new man. There are five of us, the captain in the lead. Behind him are Just and Gussmann. Scholtz and I bring up the rear. For the first time I fly the Fokker triplane. We skim over the pockmarked landscape at about five hundred meters altitude.

Above the ruins of Albert, just below the clouds, hangs an RE, a British artillery spotter. Probably ranging his batteries. We are a bit lower than he, but he apparently hasn't noticed us, because he quietly continues to circle. I exchange a quick look with Scholtz; he nods. I separate from the *staffel* and race for the "Tommy."

† Jagdgeschwader 1—Fighter Group 1.

I take him from the front. From below I dart for him like a shark and fire at short range. His engine is riddled like a sieve. He tilts over at once and disintegrates right after. The burning fragments fall close to Albert.

In another minute, I am back with the formation and continue on in the direction of the enemy. Scholtz nods at me again, quickly and happily. But the captain has noticed. He seems to have eyes everywhere. His head whips around, and he waves at me.

Below to our right is the Roman road. The trees are still bare, and through them one can see columns move. They are moving westward. British retreating before our offensive.

Just above the treetops skims a flight of Sopwith Camels. They are probably there to protect the Roman road, one of the main arteries of the British withdrawal. I hardly have time to take in the picture when Richthofen's red Fokker dives down, all of us following. The Sopwith Camels scatter like a gaggle of chickens when the hawk stabs. Only one can't get away, the one the captain has in his gunsights.

It happens so quickly, one can hardly speak of a fight. For a moment one thinks the captain might ram him, he is that close. I estimate no more than ten meters. Then the Sopwith is shaken by a blow. His nose is pushed down, a white gasoline trail appears, and he crashes in the field alongside the road in smoke and flames.

Richthofen, the steel point of our wedge formation, continues on in a steep glide toward the Roman road. At a height of about ten meters he races along the ground, both machine guns firing without letup into the marching columns on the road. We stay behind him and pour out more fire.

A paralyzing terror seems to have seized the troops; only a few make for the ditches. Most fall where they walk or stand. At the end of the road, the captain makes a tight turn and proceeds with another pass along the treetops. Now we can clearly observe the effect of our first strafing run: bolting horse teams, abandoned guns which, like breakwaters, stem the oncoming human flood.

This time we receive some return fire from below. Infantrymen stand there, rifles pressed to the cheek, and from the ditch a machine gun barks up to us. But the captain does not come up one single meter because of this, even though his wing planes are taking bullet holes. We are flying and firing close behind him. The entire *staffel* is a body subject to his will. And this is as it should be.

He leaves off the road and begins to climb. We follow. At five hundred meters we head home and land at about one o'clock. It was Richthofen's third sortie of the morning.

As my machine touches down, he is already standing on the airstrip. He comes toward me with a smile playing around his thin lips.

"Do you always bring them down with frontal attacks, Udet?" he asks. There is a hint of approval in his tone.

"I have had repeated success that way," I say as offhandedly as I can manage.

He grins again and turns to go. "By the way, you can take charge of Jasta 11 starting tomorrow," he says over his shoulder.

I already knew that I was to receive command of a *staffel,* but the form of the announcement comes as somewhat of a surprise. Scholtz slaps me on the back. "Boy, are you in with the *rittmeister.*"

"You couldn't prove it by me," I reply a bit grumbly.

But this is the way it is. One must get used to the fact that his approval will always come in an objective manner without the least trace of sentiment. He serves the idea of the Fatherland with every fiber of his being and expects nothing less from all his fliers. He judges a man by what he accomplishes to that end and also, perhaps, by his qualities as a comrade. He who passes this judgment, he backs all the way. Whoever fails, he drops without batting an eyelash. Whoever shows lukewarm on a sortie has to leave the group—on the same day.

Richthofen certainly eats, drinks, and sleeps like everyone else. But he does so only to fight. When food supplies run short, he sends Bodenschatz, the very model of an adjutant, to the rear in a squadron hack to requisition what is needed. On these occasions, Bodenschatz takes along an entire collection of autographed photos of Richthofen. "Dedicated to my esteemed fighting companion," read the inscriptions. In the rear area supply rooms these photos are highly valued. At home, in the taverns, they can reduce an entire table round to respectful silence. At the group, however, sausage and ham never run out.

A few delegates from the Reichstag‡ have announced that they are coming for a visit. Toward evening they arrive in a large limousine. They proceed with great ceremony, filled with the gravity of the moment. One of them even wears tails, and when he bows, they wave like the back feathers of a wagtail. At the supper table they talk so much that a flier can get a toothache.

"When you sit in your machine, flying out to meet the enemy, *Herr Baron* . . ." begins one of them. Richthofen sits there listening with a stony face.

After a bottle of wine they speak of heroic youth and Fatherland. We sit around the table with downcast eyes. Without finding the words, we feel that such things should not be overly much talked about. Then the gentlemen are

‡ The lower house of the German national legislature.

shown to their sleeping quarters. They sleep in the small, corrugated shacks, just like the rest of us. In this way they'll be able to report their impressions from up front back home.

We stand around in groups until the lights are dimmed behind the small windows. "Actually," says Maushacke, called "Mousetooth," "we should give them an opportunity to experience a little more of the war, since they're only going to be here until tomorrow." Scholtz winks with his right eye and says laconically: "Air raid," nothing else. We understand at once.

A ladder is brought and carefully placed against the hut in which the delegates are sleeping. Silent as a cat, Wolff clambers up to the chimney with Very pistols and blank detonating ammunition, called fliers' fards.

From the interior of the hut comes a rattling, crackling, and the hollow bang of a detonation. Immediately after, a lot of shouting. The moon is full. We stand in the dark shade of the other huts as the door opens and three shapes in flapping white nightshirts emerge. The captain laughs until tears run down his cheeks. "Aerial attack! Back into the huts," thunders a stentorian voice out of the night, and the three shapes disappear behind the door again at a dead run.

Next morning, they are in a hurry to go on. They aren't even having breakfast with us. We continue to laugh for a long time. Fun is thinly sown out here, and once a prank hits the bull's-eye, we continue to laugh for a long time. Even later, near the end of the war, when we fought like drowning swimmers, this did not change.

I think of our prisoner in Bernes. Lothar von Richthofen, the captain's brother, has brought down another one. He's an English major, and he came down just alongside our encampment. There is no infantry near, so we keep the prisoner with us.

At supper, he appears at the casino with Richthofen and is presented to everyone. He's a long drink of water, a bit fancy, but sporting in appearance. He affects a courteous reserve; in short, a gentleman. We talk about horses, dogs, and airplanes. We don't talk of the war. The Englishman is our guest, and we don't want to give him the impression that he is being pumped for information.

In the middle of the conversation he whispers to his neighbor, then he rises and walks out.

Lothar looks after him, a bit worried.

"Where is he going?"

"'I beg your pardon, where is the W.C.?' he asked," replies Mousetooth.

For a moment there is an embarrassed silence. The little hut in question is almost three minutes distant at the end of the ravine in which the camp is located. Beyond it are the woods. It will not be difficult for an athlete to reach freedom from there.

There are conflicting opinions. Maushacke, the well-fed Brunswicker, is the most enterprising. He wants to go out and stand alongside the Englishman. This could be done without too much ado. But Lothar disagrees. "We have treated the man as a guest thus far and he has done nothing to cast doubt on his good manners." But the tension remains. After all, we are responsible for the prisoner. If he gets away, there'll be hell to pay.

Someone steps to the window to look after the Englishman. In seconds six or eight are grouped around him. I'm there too. The Englishman walks across the open ground in long strides. He stops, lights a cigarette, and looks around. All of us immediately sink into a deep knee bend. Our hospitality is sacred, and our suspicion might offend him.

He disappears behind the pineboards of the outhouse. The

boards don't reach to the ground, and we can see his brown boots. This is reassuring.

But Maushacke's suspicions are awakened.

"Boys," he yaps almost breathlessly, "he no longer stands in his boots. He has gone over the rear wall in his stocking feet and is off and gone. The boots couldn't stand like this at all, if . . ."

He demonstrates to how the boots should be deployed during this kind of business.

The Englishman reappears from behind the wall. Bent low, we creep back to our seats. As he re-enters, we talk of horses, dogs, and airplanes.

"I would never forgive myself for disappointing such hosts," says the English major with a small smile around the corners of his mouth. We thank him seriously and ceremoniously.

Next morning, a short, bushy-bearded reservist calls for the prisoner, who turns around often to wave at us.

Five days later Meyer brings curious news from Ghent. An Englishman has overpowered his guard and escaped in a German uniform. From the toilet of a moving express train. His guard was found there, locked in.

"Was it a major?" asks Mousetooth excitedly.

"Are you clairvoyant?" asks Meyer. "It sure was, an Air Force major."

"So, he used the W.C. after all," shouts Mousetooth.

Meyer looks around with surprise. We all laugh until our jaws ache.

Sometimes we fly alone, sometimes with the entire *staffel*, but we fly every day. Almost every day brings a fight. On March 28 I am under way with Gussmann. A patrol toward Albert. It is afternoon, and the sun already stands in the west. Its glaring light bites at the eyes. From time to time, the light must be screened off with the thumb so that the horizon may be searched for the enemy. Otherwise you'll be surprised. The late Guynemer has taught his lessons to the entire front. Suddenly, an Englishman is above us anyway. He comes down on Gussmann, who avoids him by diving. A hundred meters below I see them maneuvering around. I watch for a spot where I can take the Englishman without hitting Gussmann.

I lift my head for a moment and see a second Englishman making for me. He is barely 150 meters off. At eighty meters he opens fire. It is impossible to avoid him, so I go straight toward him. Tack . . . tack . . . tack bellows mine at him, tack . . . tack . . . tack bellows his back at me.

We are still twenty meters apart, and it looks as though we will ram each other in another second. Then, a small movement, and he barely skims over me. His propwash shakes me, and the smell of castor oil flows past me.

I make a tight turn. "Now begins the dogfight," I think. But he has also turned, and again we come at each other, firing like two tournament knights with lances at rest. This time I fly over him.

Another bank. Again, he is straight across from me, and once more we go for each other. The thin, white trails of the tracers hang in the air like curtains. He skims over me with barely a hand's width to spare . . . "8224" it says on his fuselage in black numerals.

The fourth time. I can feel my hands getting damp. That fellow over there is a man who is fighting the fight of his life. Him or me . . . one of us has to go . . . there is no other way. For the fifth time! The nerves are taut to the bursting point, but the brain works coldly and clearly. This time the decision must fall. I line him up in my sights and go for him. I am resolved not to give an inch.

A flash of memory! I saw a dogfight at Lens. Two machines went for each other and collided head on. The fuselages went down in a ball of metal, fused together, and the wings continued on alone for quite a piece before they fluttered to the ground.

We come at each other like mad boars. If he keeps his nerve, we will both be lost!

Then, he turns off to avoid me. At this moment he is caught by my burst. His aircraft rears, turns on its back, and disappears in a gigantic crater. A fountain of earth, smoke. . . . Twice I circle around the impact area. Field gray§ shapes are standing below, waving at me, shouting.

I fly home, soaked through and through, and my nerves are still vibrating. At the same time, there is a dull, boring pain in my ears.

I have never thought about the opponents I have brought down. He who fights must not look at the wounds he makes. But this time I want to know who the other guy was. Toward evening, at dusk, I drive off. A field hospital is close to where I shot him down, and they will have probably brought him there.

I ask for the doctor. His white gown shines ghostly in the glaring light of the carbide lamp. The pilot had received a head shot and died instantaneously. The doctor hands me his wallet. Calling cards: Lieutenant Maasdorp, Ontario RFC 47." A picture of an old woman and a letter. "You mustn't fly so many sorties. Think of your father and me."

A medic brings me the number of the aircraft. He had cut it out, and it is covered with a fine spray of blood flecks. I drive back to the *staffel*. One must not think about the fact that a mother will cry for every man one brings down.

During the following days, the ear pains become worse. It

§ *Feld grau,* the uniform of the German soldier.

is as though one were chiseling and boring within my head. One April 6, I bring down another one. A Sopwith Camel taken out of the middle of an enemy gaggle. It is my twenty-fourth victory.

As I land, I am so overcome by pain I can hardly walk. Richthofen stands on the airstrip, and I stumble past him without salute toward the quarters.

We only have a hospital corpsman. The group has not yet been authorized a doctor. The corpsman is a nice, heavy-set guy, but I don't have too much faith in his medical competence. He digs around my ear with his instruments so I think he wants to saw open my head. "The back of the ear is filled with pus," he finally pronounces.

The door opens, and the captain enters.

"Udet, what's the matter with you?" he asks. The corpsman explains.

The captain pats me on the shoulder: "Now be gone with you, Udet."

I protest: "Maybe it'll go away."

But he cuts me off: "You'll take off tomorrow. Out here you have to be healthy."

It is hard for me to leave my new *staffel,* to interrupt my success. He knows this, because we all more or less believe in the Rule of the Series.¶ Because of this he escorts me to the two-seater himself next morning. He stands on the airstrip and waves at me with his cap. His blond hair glistens in the sun.

¶ The belief that it broke one's luck to interrupt a streak of victories.

HOMECOMING

The train arrives in Munich early in the morning. The city is still asleep, the streets are almost empty, the stores closed, and only here or there the snarl of shades being drawn up. I amble along Kaufingerstrasse, past Stachus. "Home again," I think, "back home." But the feeling of home, the warm familiarity with the things about, still eludes me. A city at dawn is as remote as a person asleep.

I go into a cigarette shop and phone my father at his office. In spite of the early hour, he is already there. He holds much store in always being the first in the office.

"Ernie," he says, and I hear him take a few deep breaths, "Ernie, you are here?"

Then we arrange not to let mother know and that I will call for him at the factory shortly before lunchtime. First, I want to see a doctor.

It is our old family doctor, and he receives me with a booming hello. With many, this may be a professional touch, but with him it comes from the bottom of his big generous heart. Then he examines me and becomes serious.

"Finished with flying, young man," he says, "your eardrum is gone and the inner ear infected."

"That's impossible." In spite of all efforts I can't prevent my voice from shaking.

"Well," he pats me on the shoulder, "perhaps Uncle Otto can patch this thing together again. It would be better if we would stay on the ground, though."

The visit has depressed me. On the way to my father, I can't shake my thoughts. No more flying—that can't be so. This would be like putting black glasses on me, to let

me wander around for the rest of my life. Then it's better
to see for a few more years and then be blind forever. I
resolve to follow the advice of the doctor only so long as I
decide it is best for me as far as I am concerned.

And then I meet my father. As soon as I step into his
office, he comes out from behind his desk and toward me in
big strides. "Boy, my dear boy," he says and stretches both
hands out to me. For a moment we stand and look at each
other, and then he speaks, a bit breathlessly.

So Sergeant Barlet's Winchester, a bit of booty, had reached
him safely and he had already taken it hunting twice.

How simple it is for men in France. They know no embarrassment when they say hello or good-bye. They embrace
and press bearded kisses into each other's face, regardless of
where they walk or stand. I have often observed this in railroad stations. We sit across from each other, separated by
the desktop. "By the way, you wrote me the other day about
a Caudron you couldn't bring down. Maybe the machine
was armored?"

I shake my head.

"But, yes, you wouldn't know," he continues intently. "I
thought we should also armor our planes, at least the cockpit
and the motor. Then the greatest danger for the pilot would
be alleviated."

I disagree. For the artillery "rabbits" this may be all right,
but for a fighter it would be completely out of the question.
With a crate thus armored, one certainly couldn't climb above
one thousand meters.

"That doesn't matter. The main business is the safety of the
pilot."

"But Dad," I say a bit loftily, "what strange ideas you
have about flying."

The enthusiastic zeal in his face flags. "Yes, you are probably right," he says in a tired voice, and at the same moment I feel a rueful shame come up within me. How little I understood him. The armor had been forged in his heart to protect me, and I had tossed it onto the scrap heap without even looking at it.

"At Krupp's they are supposedly trying out a new light metal that is bulletproof," I say in an attempt to pick up the lost thread, but he waves me off: "Let it lie, son. Let's call Mother to let her know I'm bringing a guest so she'll set an extra place on the dinner table."

And then we are home. Father walks into the room ahead of me. Mother is setting the table. I hear the clatter of the silver and then her voice: "Did you read the Army report? Our Ernie has shot down his twenty-fourth."

I can no longer hold back. I run into the room. She throws the silver onto the table, and we are in each other's arms. Then she takes hold of my head and holds me at arm's length: "Sick, son?"

"Oh, only a little bit in the ears."

She calms down immediately. This is singular about her: She is absolutely certain that nothing untoward is going to happen to me in this war, and she insists upon this with a certainty as though God had made her a personal promise, sealed with a handshake. Sometimes it makes me smile, sometimes I am touched by the innocent trust in her belief, but slowly her confidence crosses over to me, and I often believe myself that the bullet has not been cast for me this time.

We eat. In between she plies me with questions, and I answer with discretion. I don't speak of my fight with Maasdorp. I don't want to disquiet father, but I am also held back by an unaccountable aversion. Across sauerbraten and dumplings I cannot speak of a man who was all man with a hero's heart and who fell through my doing.

Yes, now I am home. One is immersed into this feeling like a warm bath. Everything relaxes, one sleeps late, eats much, and gets spoiled. I rarely go to town during the first days. What should I do there? My buddies are in the Army, many already dead, and I don't feel like strolling among strangers.

But I should really go see old Bergen. But I dread this visit. The old man is said to have become a depressive since he received the news of his son Otto's crash. What can I say to console him? It is easier to fight than to stand by idly to look at the wounds wrought by the war.

I have to go to the doctor every day. He is not very happy with the healing process. I let him talk now; it no longer touches me like it did the first time. One morning, just as I return from one of my visits, I meet Lo* in the Hofgarten. We had known each other from the old days as youngsters know one another. We had danced together a few times and had been on picnics in company with others.

We walk along together. In her delicately patterned silk dress she looks as though she had blossomed just this morning. When one looks at her, one can hardly believe that there can be such a thing as war. But then she tells me that she is working as an auxiliary nurse in an Army hospital. In her station lies a man with a bullet in his spine who has been dying for months. Every few weeks, his relatives make a long trip to see him, take leave of him, and he continues to live on. But he must die, so all the doctors say.

She looks at me with surprise, as I interrupt her curtly: "Wouldn't you rather talk about something else?"

For a while she is offended. She pushes out her lower lip and looks like a child who just had a chocolate bar taken away

* An old girl friend whose name was painted on his Fokker D VII and Fokker Dr 1 Triplane.

from it. In front of her house we make up and make a date for an evening at the Ratskeller.

In the afternoon I go to Bergen's. The maid leads me into the living room where old Bergen sits behind a newspaper. He is all by himself. Hans and Claus are in the field, and his wife died a long time ago. He lets the paper sink and looks at me over his pince-nez. His face has become startlingly old and withered, his Van Dyke hangs like a snowy icicle.

How helpless is one before the pain of another. "I wanted to . . ." I stammer . . . "because of Otto . . ."

"Let it be, Ernst, you wanted to look up Otto once more." He gets up and shakes my hand. "Come."

He opens the door and precedes me up the stairs. We stand in Otto's room, the little mansard Otto occupied as a student.

"So," says old Bergen with a flitting wave of the hand, "you can see everything here."

Then he turns around and walks out. His footfall diminishes down the stairs. I am alone with Otto.

In the little room, everything is as it was then. On the chest and on the book shelves stand model airplanes that Otto had built himself. They look beautiful, these models. All the types known at that time, reproduced to the most minute detail. But when they flew, they fell like stones. That was ten years ago.

I step up to the children's desk with the green, ink-spotted cover and fold up the top. They are still there, the composition books, the diary of the Aero Club Munich, 1909. Its members were between ten and thirteen years old. Every Wednesday there was a model building group in our attic, every Saturday a big airplane meet by the Stadtbach or the Isar. Otto's planes were always the most beautiful, but mine, ugly sparrows though they were, flew farthest. Somehow, I had the knack. And in his neat, child's handwriting he had noted down everything in his capacity as secretary of the club. "The aviator, *Herr* Ernst Udet, was awarded first prize for the successful channel crossing of his model U-11" it says there, because my type had gotten across the Isar without accident.

Everything is so neatly placed, as though he had arranged everything before taking his final leave. There are letters, all the letters I had written to him, packed in small bundles and marked with the year they were written. On top is the last, unopened. In it, there is news that I have finally succeeded in getting him released for my *staffel*. The letter closes: "Hurrah, Otto!"

There are the drawings. He always did the right half, I the left. The photographs all are there, beginning with those from earliest childhood. He has even saved the ones from the "Meet at Niederschau." I jumped with the first glider constructed by the Aero Club and cracked up. The bird broke its beak and Willi Goetz, our chairman, informed the people of Niederschau that the ground magnetism in the area was too strong for flying. Then, group shots from the first days of dancing school loves, then the war, motorcyclists, the first flying suits, after the first victory. Under each photo the date and in neat lettering the caption in white ink. He had lived my life with me.

There is something strange about the friendship of boys. We would have rather bitten our tongues than to admit even by a single word that we cared for each other. Only now do I see it all before me.

I close the desk and go down the stairs. Old Bergen again sits behind his paper. He gets up and shakes my hand; there is no pressure, no warmth.

"If you want some of Otto's things, Ernst," he says, "take what you like. He liked you most of all his friends."

He turns away and begins to clean his pince-nez. I have none, and a few tears run across my face. I stand in the hallway for a while before I step out into the street.

I was twenty-one then, and Otto was my best friend.

In the evening I meet Lo at the Ratskeller. I wear "civvies" because I want to forget the war for an evening. But Lo feels hurt. I don't look sufficiently heroic.

We eat tough, stringy veal and large, bluish potatoes that look as though they were anemic and had spent too much time in the water. Only the wine has ripe sweetness and gives no indication of the war.

An old lady comes by with roses. Lo glances sideways at the flowers. "Leave them be," I say in a low voice, "they're all wired anyhow."

But the old one has heard me; she puts down her basket and plants herself squarely in front of us.

"This I like fine," she shrieks in a broad Bavarian dialect and stems her arms into her hips. "Such a fine little snot sits around, all dolled up, and wants to take the bread out of the mouth of an old woman. In the trenches, that's where you belong, young man, that much I tell you."

People at the neighboring tables, their attention attracted by the old lady's clamor, are looking at us. This would be pretty embarrassing if I were a dodger but, since I'm not, it amuses me, but Lo has blushed to the roots of her hair.

"Well," I say, "so give me a couple of bundles."

The transformation is miraculous. Her ire has passed with the speed of a theater storm, and her face is suffused with sweetness and courtesy. She hastily fishes around among her bundles of roses.

"Never mind me, young man," she babbles on, "anyone can see you are still much too young to go out. I just let my temper run away with me. All you have to do is look to see," she says, turning to the people at the surrounding tables, "any child can tell that this boy just celebrated his confirmation."

I wave her off. Lo has an ominous wrinkle between her eyebrows.

"Just confirmed," she snaps.

I reach for her small, sun-tanned hand, lying on the white tablecloth.

"You know," I say, "just once, I would like to be alone with you, away from everything." It is an attack straight out of the sun. She is so surprised, I can almost read the thoughts behind the round, childlike forehead.

"We would have to drive out," I said, "somewhere in the country. Perhaps we could go to Lake Starnberg; Gustav Otto has invited me. Perhaps we could also go farther up into the mountains. We could be free and unencumbered and enjoy nature, as though we were in another world."

At first she smiles, then she purses her lips.

"But we could hardly do this. What would my parents say?"

"Please forgive me," I say, "but I have left my manners in the field."

We go. It is a humid night, and the wind rustles the tree-tops. We stop under a lantern, and she pats me on the arm.

"Please don't be angry."

I shrug: "Angry? No!"

But I feel something is amiss. Out in the field, everything has changed. Things that were once important are no longer of any value. Other things as important as life itself. But back here, life has stood still. I can't put it into words, but suddenly I feel homesick for my buddies.

We stop at the garden gate in front of Lo's home. She lingers, but I quickly kiss her hand quite correctly and make a fast getaway.

On the next day I go out by myself. I'm in a rotten mood. I can't get back to the front. When I brought up the subject, the doctor read me the riot act. But back here I feel lost. When I come home, my parents are already asleep.

On one evening, however, all windows are still alight. I run up the stairs as the door opens and my mother stands on the jamb, her face red and shining with happiness. She is waving a piece of paper in her hand, a telegram from the group, advising that I had been awarded the *Pour le Mérite*.

I am happy, really happy, even though it doesn't come as a complete surprise. After a certain number of victories, the *Pour le Mérite* comes—it is almost automatic. But the real joy is that which reflects from my mother. She is beside herself and has kept everyone up to wait for me, even my little sister. She has cut a medal out of paper and now hangs it around my neck with a piece of yarn.

My father shakes hands with me. "Congratulations, son," he says, nothing else. But he has opened a bottle of Steinberger Kabinett, 1884 vintage, one of the family heirlooms. This says more than words. The wine is golden yellow and flows like oil. Its fragrance permeates the entire room. We touch glasses.

"To peace, a good peace," says father.

Next morning, in bed, I think of Lo. If I had my *Pour le Mérite*, I would make a date with her, as if nothing had happened. I jump out of bed, get dressed, and go into town.

I go to an orders jeweler on Theatinerstrasse. The salesman shrugs his shoulders: *"Pour le Mérite?—*No! Insufficient demand." Too bad. I thought I could surprise Lo. But it will be at least two weeks before the medal will reach me from my unit. Slowly I amble along the street, mechanically returning salutes to soldiers and officers passing by. There

comes a naval officer; it is Wenninger, commander of a submarine. At his throat, a *Pour le Mérite* glistens in the sun.

It is the inspiration of the moment. I go toward him,
saluting, and ask: "Excuse me, but do you per chance happen
to have a second *Pour le Mérite?*"

He gives me a wide-eyed look, and I explain. He laughs
loudly and embarrassingly long. No, he doesn't have a second
one, but he gives me the address of a store in Berlin where
I can order one, by telegram if I so desire. I thank him, a
little chagrined, and salute formally.

Two days later, the order arrives from Berlin. It lies like
a star in a red velvet case. I give Lo a call to make a date.
She laughs and accepts at once. Waiting for her, I parade up
and down in front of her house. Then she comes and spots
the order around my neck at once. "Ernie," she shouts, and
comes hopping along like a bird trying to take off. In the
middle of the street, in front of everyone, she throws here
arms around my neck and kisses me.

It is a bright, sunny, spring morning. Side by side, we
walk slowly and loose-jointed toward the center of town.
When soldiers pass, they salute especially sharply, and most
turn around. Lo counts: Out of forty-three, twenty-seven have
turned around. We walk along Theatinerstrasse, the main
artery of Munich, from which life seems to radiate and where
it returns. In front of the Residenz† stands the sentry, a short
reservist with bristling beard and button nose. Suddenly,
with a voice of proportions unexpected from such a small
chest, he shouts:

"The Guard, fall out!"

The men come piling out. "Fall in," commands the officer.
"Left shoulder arms! *Achtung!* Present arms!"

I look around. There is no one else near. Then I remember

† The home of the King of Bavaria.

my *Pour le Mérite*. I am almost past when I return the salute. It comes off a bit small, too hasty and without dignity.

"What was that all about?" asks Lo, looking at me with big eyes.

"God," I say loftily, "before a *Pour le Mérite,* the Guard has to fall out."

"You're kidding!"

"No, I'm not!"

"Good, then we'll try once more."

At first I object a little, but I finally give in. After all, I'm still not all that certain myself.

This time we are well prepared and enter into this affair with good posture. "Guards, fall out," shouts the sentry. At the same moment Lo hooks into my arm and, with a gracious nod, she troops the short line at my side.

Woman's vanity is insatiable. If she had her way, we would spend the rest of the afternoon chasing the Guard in and out. But I go on strike. The Guard detail is no toy for little girls. Lo pouts.

They are days of blue silk. Never again did I experience such a spring. We meet every day, strolling through the English Garden, drinking tea or going to the theater. The war is far, far away. Once we see a crowd near the theater, gathering around a poster on the wall.

"Probably news of another victory," I say, as we walk up.

But in reading the poster I feel as though someone had struck a blow at my heart. *"Rittmeister Freiherr* von Richthofen missing!" it says. The letters wave uncertainly in front of my eyes. I see no one and pay attention to no one as I elbow my way through the crowd to get close. Fifty centimeters in front of me, the yellowish-white piece of paper bears the message: "Did not return from a mission. Investigations without result at this time."

Then I know for certain, the captain is dead.

What a man he was. Certainly, the others fought too. But they had wives or children, a mother or a profession. This they could forget only on rare occasions. But he constantly lived beyond those boundaries that we only cross during great moments. His personal life was blotted out when he fought at the front. And he always fought when he was at the front. Food, drink, and sleep was all he was willing to concede to life. Only that which was necessary to keep that machine of flesh and blood going. He was the least complicated man I ever knew. Entirely Prussian and the greatest of soldiers.

A hand carefully pushes into mine. For seconds I had completely forgotten Lo.

"If you still want to take that drive into the country, I'll gladly come with you," she says, looking at me as though I were condemned to die tomorrow.

On the next day we're off to Lake Starnberg. The leaves break out early this year; trees and bushes are already frothy with bright green. We stay with Gustav Otto and his wife. They are simple and open-hearted people. They know and respect the first rule of hospitality. They don't force us to fit into their routine and let us go on just as we please. During the mornings we ride or row on the lake; in the afternoon we stroll through the woods. We wade through the wilted leaves of the last fall, while overhead the new green already blossoms on the branches. It really seems as though there were no war. When all of us are dead and forgotten, these trees will continue to green, bear fruit, and wilt.

And yet, yet . . . sometimes, when we lie there on our backs in the grass, I catch myself scanning the thick bellies of the cumulus clouds above. Perhaps one will come diving out of those clouds? And in the mornings, when I rise, my first look is skyward. What is the flying weather like?

During the first five days I did not even read a newspaper, but now I already walk a few paces to meet the mailman. It must be wild out there. The group is in the thick of it, and Loewenhardt brings one down almost every day. He has now reached thirty-seven, and when I left we have just pulled even. We probably also have serious losses. It is noon, and Lo and I are in the boat in the middle of the lake.

"You know," I say thoughtfully, "sometimes I wish I was back out there again." It is the first time I mention this.

Lo lets go of the rudder line and stares at me, her lips shaking.

"Well then, you have so little love for me?"

No, she didn't understand. I get up and sit aft. The boat rocks mightily. I give her a kiss. I am a little sad; my mother would have understood at once.

The weather is unbelievably beautiful. Each day more so than the last. During the third week I go to Munich to see the doctor. The inflammation has abated. "But we'll need re-cuperation, young man, recuperation," he says complacently.

Evenings we sit on the terrace of Gustav Otto's house. The moon is full. Lo is tired and goes to her room early. I sit in a reclining chair next to Gustav Otto. We are smoking.

"Would you be very angry if one morning I would suddenly be up and gone?"

By the fiery disk of his cigar I can tell that he has turned his head toward me.

"What does the doctor say?"

"He's satisfied, so far."

He is silent for a while. Then: "I think that's the way I would do it."

"Good." We understand one another.

At five in the morning, Otto wakens me, and we sneak down the stairs on tiptoes. Lo is still asleep, and the car is waiting below.

The station is almost empty at this hour. Only a few women going to market. It looks like rain. The first gray day in weeks. The morning has trouble rising over the hills.

I return to the front.

THE END

The group is stationed at Monthussart-Ferme. I arrive toward noon and go straight to the mess. There are many new faces, clicking heels, mumbled names. At the table, there are many reunions. Gluczewski, Maushacke, Rauter von Prestin's blond head, Drekmann, hellos, nods, toasts. Sometimes, the eyes seek in vain, but those missing are not discussed.

After lunch, Reinhard takes me aside. He carries the group cane, the cane of the dead captain, which is supposed to be inherited by each new commander.

"You already know, Udet?"

I nod.

"If you want, we can go and have a look."

It is a midsummer day, quiet. The poplars by the road vibrate in the heat like molten glass. The car moves quietly along the road. On a small hill to the right, a churchyard. We get out and, Reinhard in front, go through the wrought iron gate onto the narrow paths between the graves.

There are four mounds of fresh earth, four square tablets and, above these, a cross fashioned of broken propellers. "Pilot-Corporal Robert Eisenbeck, Lieutenant Hans Weiss, Lieutenant Edgar Scholtz, Lieutenant Joachim Wolff," it says on the tablets.

Reinhard salutes; I salute.

"They had a good death," he says.

We stand there for a long while, then we return to the group.

Things have changed out here. The French fly only in large units—fifty, sometimes a hundred aircraft. They darken the skies like locusts. Hard to knock one out of these formations.

The artillery on the other side now also works mostly with aerial observation. The balloons stand on the horizon in long rows, and observers circle incessantly above the crater-torn landscape. The troops suffer much. . . .

I am still in bed when the phone rings. Drunk with sleep, I fish for the receiver. An artillery captain from up front. North of the woods near Villers-Cotterets there is a Breguet directing the enemy artillery. The effect is terrible.

"Where is that?"

He reads off the coordinate from the staff map.

"We'll be there!" I hang up.

The others are all gone, and I am off duty this morning, but there haven't been any regular hours for some time. We take off whenever it's necessary.

In five minutes I'm ready and take off. The front is going wild on this day. Grenades impact so closely together that the smoke, dust, and fountains of earth form a curtain, shutting out the sun. The landscape below me is obscured by a pale brown haze.

North of the woods of Villers-Cotterets I meet the Breguet at an altitude of about six hundred meters. I immediately attack him from the rear at the same altitude.

In a Breguet, the observer sits behind the pilot. I can clearly see his head above the ring mount of his machine gun. But he can't fire as long as I stay directly behind him. Stabilizer and rudder obscure his view.

My machine gun barks a short burst. The head disappears from above the ring mount. "Hit," I think.

The pilot of the Breguet seems to be a smart boy. Although I keep him under constant fire, he makes an elegant turn with his clumsy bird and attempts to make for his own lines. I have to take him from the side in order to get him or the engine. If the observer were still alive, this would be a bad mistake, because I would fly straight into his field of fire.

I have closed in to about twenty meters when the observer appears behind his machine gun, ready to fire. In a moment it rattles about my head as though pebbles were falling onto a metal tabletop. "Gontermann!" I think. My Fokker rears like a shying horse and turns into a sitting duck. The elevator is shot up, its binding at the stick is severed, and the cable flaps in the propwash.

My machine is shot lame, drooping to the left and circling, always circling. I can't steer it. Below me is the torn landscape, being turned over anew by the impact of new shells. There is only one possibility to get back. Every time the Fokker heads east, I carefully open the throttle. In this way the circles are elongated, and I can hope to work my way back to our lines.

It is a slow, tortuous process. Suddenly, the machine stands on end and dives straight down like a rock.

Parachute—pull up the legs—stand on the seat! In a moment the air pressure throws me to the rear. A blow in my back. I'm stuck to the rudder. The straps of the parachute harness, secured too loosely, have become fouled with the equalization flap, and the falling machine is dragging me along with irresistible force. "Lo will cry . . ." I think, "Mother . . . I will be unrecognizable . . . have no papers on me . . . they're shooting like mad down there . . ." At the same time I attempt, with all my strength, to bend back the flap. It is hard, terribly hard. The ground is coming at me fast. Then—a jerk—I am free! The machine drops off below me. A sharp pull, and I float on the straps like a swimmer. Immediately after, a jolt, and I have landed. The parachute opened at the last moment.

The parachute billows above me. Around me, the cracking impacts of artillery shells. I fight against the white cloth wall like a drowning man. Finally I get myself loose. The crater landscape is bleak. I must be between the lines, but I don't know where. I'll have to go east; that's home. It is about eight in the morning, and the sun is pale, as though it were burned out. Down here, the curtain of dust caused by the shell bursts is even more dense.

I unhook the parachute and start running. The shell bursts come closer, as though they were racing toward me. A large clod of earth hits me in the back of the head like a fist. I fall down, clamber back up, and continue running. My right leg hurts. It must have been sprained when I touched down.

A crater and a few French helmets. Am I still behind the enemy lines? The soldiers facing east are showing me their backs. They aren't moving. Perhaps they are dead. I'll be better if I go around them. I go into a wheat field. The stalks are already approaching the height of a man. I run in a crouch and go up a gentle incline rising eastward.

The field is quite long, but it finally comes to an end. I take a look around through the green curtain of the stalks. An officer stands there, erect.

"First . . . fire!" he commands, and is answered by the roar of a gun. I stand up and wave at him. He waves back, and I run toward him.

"Cigarette?" I say with dry lips. "Bayer," he introduces himself, salutes, and produces a cigarette case. "Udet," I say, and for a moment the drumfire doesn't exist, so strong are the rituals of upbringing that even the war can't obliterate.

"Second ready?" he shouts. "Ready!" comes the retort from the dugouts.

"Second . . . fire!" The ground is shaken by the detonation.

1. The "Aeroclub 1909" peeping through the fence of the Otto Works.

2. Volunteer flyer with Lieutenant Justinius.

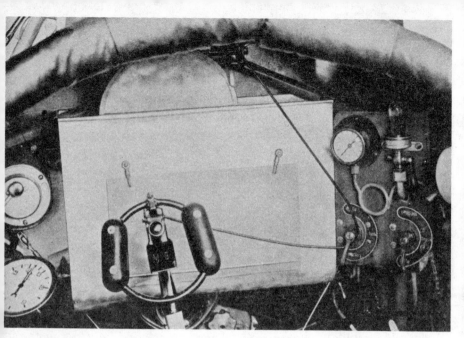

3. The blocked steering that caused the mishap with the Fokker.

4. Single-Seater Combat Command Habsheim.
From the left: Pfaelzer, Weingaertner, Udet, Glinkermann.

5. The "Nieuport target" mock-up for my aerial gunnery practice.

6. Albatros D III with mechanics Behrend and Guntelmann.

7. "The silent observer." To mislead the enemy, a tin head was mounted on my Fokker.

8. Glinkermann, shortly before his last flight.

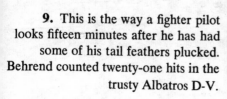

9. This is the way a fighter pilot looks fifteen minutes after he has had some of his tail feathers plucked. Behrend counted twenty-one hits in the trusty Albatros D-V.

10. C.O. of Jasta 37. Flanders, 1917.

11. Lothar and Manfred von Richthofen.

12. On standby,
waiting for the "Tommies."

13. Richthofen, shortly before his last flight on April 21, 1918.
From the left: Wolfram von Richthofen, Scholtz, Carjus, Wolff, Luebbert,
Manfred von Richthofen, Lowenhardt, Just, Weiss.

14. Arrogance precedes the
downfall—the machine from
which I was forced to
bail out on the next day.
(The inscription is commonly
translated as "Not you,"
which, although literal, does
not express its meaning, which
is the idiomatic equivalent
of "You and who else?")

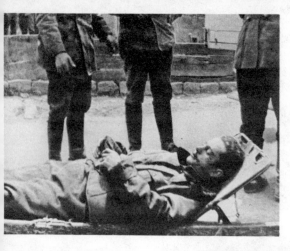

15. The American, Lieutenant Wanamaker, wounded on a stretcher, after being shot down.

16. From then on, my aircraft was named *Lo*.

17. Udet's quarters with the Richthofen group.

He lights a match for me, and I inhale the smoke in long, hungry drags.

"Observed your jump, *Herr* Kamerad; that was something. Third ready?"

I ask him for directions to the rear positions. He points over his back toward the heights of Cutry.

I thank him and limp on. A new fire zone and, again, the impacts are coming close to me. Once, I am flung to the ground by the blast of a burst.

A dugout with a burning fire in front, protection against gas. Inside the dugout a confusion of officers and men. I turn to a telephone operator to ask him to connect me with the group.

"Udet," someone shouts behind me, "it's Ernie!" I turn around and look at a strange soldier. His hard, pale face with the red-rimmed eyes tells of many hard days and wakeful nights.

"Carl Moser?" I say hesitantly.

"That's who." Under his direction I welded the first pipes together at my father's factory.

"Do you remember . . . do you remember the time . . . ?" The world around us becomes remote. We stand on a grassy field, three boys, Willi Goetz, Otto Bergen, and I. Carl is lying on his back in his Sunday best, chewing a leaf of grass, watching us flying kites.

A little girl accompanies the launching of each kite with gleeful handclapping. Willi Goetz grabs her, five kites are tied together and she tied to them, and up she goes. She shrieks like a stuck suckling, and her mother comes running. We all take off; only Otto remains behind. Slowly and carefully, he pulls the kites back down. The woman cries and slaps him from time to time, but he doesn't let go of the cord.

"Where is Otto now?" asks Carl.

"Dead!" I say.

"Hm, also dead," he mumbles.

My call comes through. The group car will pick me up at the road from Soissons to Château Thierry. I am supposed to get there on a horse borrowed from the regimental staff.

Late in the afternoon I go up again with a new machine. Among the craters below I see the Fokker in which I crashed that morning. The ribbing, burned bare, sticks up into the air. It looks like the skeleton of a bird.

The war gets tougher by the day. When one of our aircraft rises, five go up on the other side. And when one of theirs comes down near us, we fall on him and strip him bare because we have long run out of such fine instruments, shining with nickel and brass. Against this affluence we can pit nothing more than our sense of duty and the experience of four long years. Each takeoff means a fight now, and we take off often. During the time from the third to the twenty-fifth of August I bring down twenty opponents.

On one of the dead men my picture, cut from a newspaper, is found with the caption: *"As des As."** The captain is dead, and I now have the largest score.

On the afternoon of the eighth, the order comes for the group to move up to the Somme with all available machines. There, the English have been battling for a breakthrough for several days. Things are supposed to be critical for us. Four swarms of large birds of prey, we roar northward. The farther north we get, the more the landscape below us shows the marks of battle. Near Fontaine les Cappy I discover an enemy aircraft on contact patrol, skimming over the trenches. I separate myself from the *staffel* and stab at him, firing as I

* French for "Ace of Aces."

go. After twenty rounds he bursts in the air and disintegrates alongside the trenches. It is 5:30 P.M.

At about six we begin to run low on fuel. We did not have much when we took off. Supplies were short during the last few days, and no one expected such a long flight. We have to land to gas up. Below us is a small airfield. We drop down like starlings into a wheat field. One machine lines up next to the other. The field is packed.

The *staffel* commanders have themselves announced to the commandant of the field, an amiable fellow. He would like to help us but, after all, he needs gasoline for his own aircraft. We suggest that he share his supply with us. He hesitates.

While we negotiate, the air is filled with the rumble of British motors. During their approach, we can already smell the odor of castor oil wafting our way. Here and there a swarm appears briefly in the openings between clouds. It is a cool summer evening. The heavy clouds have moved off to the east, pulling the remaining fragments after them. The blue of the sky shows through only in spots. "Good weather for balloon attacks," I say to myself.

Suddenly, a British machine darts out of the gray haze above us, firing at our machines from both barrels. It is a sorry sight. The Richthofen group, herded together here like a gaggle of hens, helpless without gas, and above it a hawk, the Englishman. I am seized by a raging anger. I race to my aircraft and take off without being strapped in.

He makes another pass at us, and I go at him from below. He is so surprised, he neglects to defend himself. Only ten rounds and he staggers and crashes close by the airfield. Dead.

It was a British S.E. 5, with the streamers of a leader. I land without a drop of gas and a dead stick. Time: 6:30 P.M.

We have finally gotten sufficient juice from the commandant for about a ten-minute flight. Barely enough to get us to our new destination.

We land there on an open field. During the preceding days, the British have had the entire area strafed daily by swarms of close support aircraft. Every evening between eight and nine, two Sopwith Camels come over to drop leaflets. Somebody shows me one of these things. It has a black-red-yellow border. Supposed deserters are prompting the soldiers in the trenches to do likewise.

"Between eight and nine, you say?"

I scrape together some gas from among my buddies and take off. The sun is already low in the west, framing the clouds in a pale golden color.

South of Foucaucourt I meet the two. One immediately takes off westward; the other remains. He rains leaflets on me from above. We begin to maneuver. With his smaller, lighter aircraft, he can make tighter circles than I with my heavy Fokker D VII. But I stay behind him. He tries to shake me and starts a loop from barely one hundred meters altitude. I follow on his heels, and at the apex I flash on underneath him. My turning radius is larger than his. I feel a slight blow, and when I look down again, I see him creeping laboriously from the wreckage of his aircraft. German soldiers are picking him up. I don't know what happened. The only thing I can figure is that I must have rammed him as I flew past. It was my third fight today. The clock shows eight-forty.

Three days later I visit him at the hospital in Foucaucourt. As a return favor for his leaflets, I bring him a box of cigars made from beech leaves. My surmise was correct. At the apex of the loop, my undercarriage rammed his upper wing plane, which cracked out beyond the struts. "I wasn't prepared for this kind of clinch fighting," he said laughingly. He is a nice fellow, a student from Ontario.

Fifteen years later, at a flying meet in Los Angeles, I hear from him again. Roscoe Turner brings me a leaflet on his nonstop cross-continent flight. It has a black-red-yellow border, coming from supposed deserters, addressed to the soldiers in the trenches. It is the last of his supply, and he forgot to throw it at me in 1918.

At dusk I land back at group. We spend the night on the ground, sleeping under our aircraft. We rise at daybreak. Tanks are coming!

During the night, gasoline and ammunition had been brought up. We assign our sectors and take off. I see them between Bapaume and Arras. A smoke screen is rising before them, and under its cover they creep across the flat, grassy plain. Fifteen of them, like mighty steel turtles. They creep, creep, creep.

They have already passed over the first German positions . . . the second . . . they continue to roll into the rear areas. We dive, firing with both barrels, climb, and come down again. No effect. It is like a woodpecker knocking against an iron door. The German infantry has withdrawn behind the railroad dam of the Bapaume-Arras line. It rises from the swampy grassland like a fortress wall, four meters high, covered with ballast. From there, their machine guns rattle into the laundry room haze of the artificial smoke screen. Without letup and without effect.

The turtles continue to creep. One of them has now reached the dam; it clumsily mounts the incline and rolls along the tracks. I can see our men fleeing from their positions, dragging their machine guns along. They disappear in ground folds and water ditches.

Slowly, the tank clambers along the railroad dam, spewing

his volleys after them. A new target for me. I can now go at him from the side. Hardly three meters above the ground I go for him, go right up to him, hop over him, turn, and have another go. I get so close to him that I can make out every barrel and rivet on his steel plates. Even the washed-out clover leaf on his side, either a good luck charm or a unit insignia. I hop over him again, so low that my undercarriage almost touches the hump of his turret. I swing around and go at him again.

Through this low-level tactic I neutralize the other tanks. If they fire on me, they fire on their own man.

With the fifth attack I notice the first effect. Clumsily, the tank feels its way to the edge of the dam. It wants to get back down and into the covering smoke screen. I don't let him out of my sight and follow his every move. Carefully he juts out over the edge of the dam. Now, nearly half of his plump steel body sticks out into the air. At the next moment he weaves and tumbles down the incline, landing on his back, helpless like a fallen bug.

I come down from above, hammering my bursts into his lightly armored underside. The tracks are still turning, the right snapping upward, reaching like the arm of a polyp and falling back. The tank now lies still, as if dead, but I still fire into it.

A hatch on the side of the gun turret opens. A man stumbles out, hands up in front of his bleeding face. I am so close that I can observe all this. But I can't fire any more. I have used up my ammunition to the last round.

I return to the forward airstrip, have new belts loaded up, and return. The whole thing lasted barely twenty minutes. But the tank is dead. It lies there black and motionless. Three men in the grass at its side. The British medics must have been there in the meanwhile. They pulled out the dead men and left them there. I hope they'll be buried by the next barrage.

The night comes. Fog rises from the grass. The tank attack has been beaten back. It came to a halt on the Bapaume-Arras line.

An excited voice on the telephone: "Two balloons have just been shot down here. The enemy squadron is still circling over our position."

We take off at once, the entire fourth *staffel* with all available machines. We head toward Braie at three thousand meters altitude. Below us the chain of German balloons, obliquely above us the British squadron, five S.E. 5's. We stay below them and wait for their attack. But they hang on and seem to be avoiding a fight.

Suddenly, one of them darts past me down toward the balloons. I push down and go after him. It is their leader. The narrow streamer flaps in front of me. I push down, down, down. The air screams at the windshield. I must catch him, stop him from getting to the balloons.

Too late! The shadow of his aircraft flits across the taut skin of the balloon like a fish through shallow water. A small blue flame licks out and creeps slowly across its back. At the next moment a fountain of fire shoots up where, just a moment ago, the golden yellow bag had floated with a silken glow.

A German Fokker comes at the Englishman; a second, smaller fireball lights up alongside the larger one, and the German aircraft hits the ground wrapped in smoke and flame.

In a very tight turn, the Englishman goes almost straight down. The troops at the balloon cable winch scatter, but the S.E. 5 has already flattened out and sweeps westward, hugging the ground. He is down so low that the machine and its shadow merge into one. But now I am on his tail and a wild chase begins, hardly three meters above ground. We hop telegraph poles and dodge trees. A mighty jump, the church steeple of Marécourt, but I hang on to him. I'm not about to let go.

The main highway to Arras. Flanked by high trees, it winds through the landscape like a green wall. He flies to the right of the trees, I to the left. Every time there is a gap in the trees I fire. Alongside the road, on a meadow, German infantry is encamped. Although I am on his neck, he fires at them. This is his undoing.

At that moment I jump the treetops—hardly ten meters separate us—and fire. A tremor runs through his machine; it wavers, tumbles into a spin, hits the ground, bounces up again like a stone rebounding from the water, and disappears in a mighty hop behind a small birch grove. A dust cloud rises.

Perspiration is running across my face, and it fogs my goggles. I wipe my forehead with my sleeve. It is midsummer, August 22, 12:30 P.M., the hottest day of the year. Almost forty degrees centigrade, and during the pursuit my motor ran at 1600 rpm.

I look around and see three S.E. 5's. They have shaken off my squadron and are diving on me to avenge their dead leader. Close to the ground, I chase around the birch grove. I take short, quick looks over my shoulder. They are splitting up, two turning off to the west, leaving me to one of them.

I know now that I am dealing with tactically tried and proven opponents. Beginners would have come at me in a bunch. Old fighter pilots know that during a pursuit you only get into each other's way.

Thing are looking bad for me. The other works himself in toward me. I estimate the distance at barely thirty meters, but he still does not fire. "He wants to finish me off with three or four rounds," I figure.

The landscape consists of gently rolling hills dotted with small groves. I curve around these groves. Among the trees I spot a German machine gun unit. They stare up at us. "If they would only shoot to release me from my predicament." But they don't fire. Perhaps we are too close together, perhaps they are afraid they might hit me in the constant up and down. I take in the landscape. So this is where I will fall!

Then I feel a light, dull blow at my knee. I look down and notice the sweet, faint odor of phosphorus and a hole in the ammunition case. The heat—the phosphorus ammunition has ignited itself—in a matter of seconds, my aircraft will be in flames.

In a situation like this, one doesn't think. One acts or dies. A squeeze on the machine gun trigger and from both barrels the ammunition stabs out into the blue sky, trailing white smoke.

A look over my shoulder, breathless surprise, and then a few deep, lung-filling breaths. The enemy turns away, avoiding the white smoke trails. He probably thinks I am firing backward. I fly home.

After touching down I remain seated in the cockpit for quite a while. Behrend has to help me out of the machine. I go to the orderly room.

"*Oberleutnant* Goering is coming tonight," says the sergeant. I look at him with empty eyes.

"Goering, our new C.O.," he repeats.

"Yes, yes." My own voice sounds strange to me. I want to go on furlough. At once. Right away. He must not see me this way.

When I return from leave, the group is stationed at Metz. The losses have been great. Three hundred percent have fallen. Three times, in the course of the war, the complement of officers has turned over. There is hardly anyone left who made the first flights with the captain. For this reason, the High Command has pulled us out of the hot spot and placed us in a quiet sector for a short time.

Goering is just flying a standing patrol with his *staffel* when I arrive. He lands, and we greet each other. His face is dark. He was put into Richthofen's spot because he is regarded the foremost air strategist of the Army. On this dead sector, his talent is aground, and he must fight his battles on paper.

"Hello, Udet," he mumbles.

Shortly afterward I take off with my *staffel*. Bursts on the horizon, little black clouds of German flak,† indicate enemy aircraft in sight. They are coming closer, seven aircraft, two-seaters of the De Havilland 9 type. We are six. But they are new at the front, an American formation. The youngest of us has two years of front line experience on them.

We met close to the airfield. The entire battle lasts hardly five minutes. Gluczewski brings one down, Kraut another. Mine comes down in flames near Monteningen. The others turn around and fly home. One skims along just above me. I set my Fokker on its tail and fire straight up. He can no longer avoid me. He must pass through my burst. He explodes just barely fifty meters above me, and I have to dive away fast to avoid being hit by the burning wreckage.

A third whips past me, going westward. The leader's streamer flaps from his tail. I go after him. When he notices that he is being followed, he turns around and comes at me. A burst sounds off from the other side; I feel a burning pain in my left thigh, and gasoline comes spurting out of the shot-up tank, giving me a shower.

† Antiaircraft artillery fire.

I cut the ignition and land. My buddies are crowding around. From the airfield they have been following the fight in detail. They talk in excited confusion. "Man, Udet, are you lucky . . . the first sight of the enemy in four weeks . . . returned from leave today and right away such a present . . ."

I climb out of the plane and look at my wound. The bullet passed through my thigh. It is still bleeding a little. The others step aside, and Goering comes toward me. I report: "Sixty-first and sixty-second enemy shot down. Myself slightly wounded. Shot through the left cheek, face not damaged." Goering laughs and shakes my hand.

"Nice of me to sit here and to reserve victories for you," he says as a good comrade.

And then comes the end, unbelievable for us who fought to the last. A peace none of us understand.

One day I hold in my hand a small piece of paper, my discharge.

NEW START

The man stares at me unblinkingly. He wears a gray-green soldier's coat, military cap without cockade, and a broad red band on his right sleeve. Soldier's council. From his thick cheeks the red tips of his mustache point up to his eyes like small flames. It is November 1918, a gray, rainy day. We stand on the rear platform of a crowded Munich streetcar.

The man stares and stares. Finally he sticks out his hand and points at my *Pour le Mérite*.

"That's tin," he says loudly.

Those around us look up, curious as to what will happen next. I look out of the window at the pavement, where the raindrops are bouncing, and reflect what I should do if he attacks me. But the hairy paw is already at my throat, tugging at the order:

"Don't you want to take off that little piece of tin?"

He is much bigger than I, but I have already gauged the distance. At the next moment I have his squirrelly red beard in my hands and pull at it full strength and shout: "Don't you want to take off your beard?"

He roars and strikes out madly. He hits the conductor, then other passengers, but he doesn't hit me. The platform turns into a battlefield. The conductor swings his fists like coal shovels, banging into the other's head.

At the next stop the man in the soldier's coat tumbles out. He picks himself up and shakes his fist, shouting threats after the departing streetcar. A few heavy-set onlookers laugh. But, try as I might, I fail to see any humor in the situation.

Evenings, we fliers often meet in a small tavern. The mood is dreary. We have been shunted aside and haven't found our footing in civilian life.

"You know," Greim says to me, "if one could at least fly again and look at this whole mess from above." We drink and stare straight ahead.

It is cold in the wood-paneled room. The coal supply must be nursed, and the lamps give off a weak light. The walls are covered with placards and posters, elections for the national assembly, a call for prisoner-of-war relief.

I grab Greim's arm. "We will fly again," I say, and tell him my plan.

Early next morning we go to the office of the POW relief organization. We offer to do exhibition dogfights, aerobatics, and the like. They are skeptical. All right, if we can obtain the aircraft. But that would be difficult. There are supposed to be some in Bamberg, brand new and not yet turned over.

So we drive to Bamberg. It is a cold, unfriendly morning. The machines are in an empty factory hangar, lined up side by side. They await delivery to the enemy, the wretched end. The heart bleeds at the sight of it.

We negotiate for some time with the administrator. Finally, we succeed in prying loose two aircraft. A Fokker D VII for Greim, a Fokker Parasol* for me.

Two weeks later there are posters on all the placard pillars of Munich: "The *Pour le Mérite* fliers Ritter von Greim versus First Lieutenant Ernst Udet."

Thousands come, tens of thousands. The affair is a huge success for the POW relief fund.

"Actually," says Greim, "it's a shame that we exhibit as a game here something we did in dead earnest out at the front . . ."

* Fokker D VIII.

"But we are flying again," I counter.

We continue to fly every Sunday in different places around Munich and throughout Bavaria. The people come and pay and the POW relief organization is happy with us. When we land we are surrounded by the curious, who want to know how it was out there. But when we are airborne, everything is forgotten. Greim is an equal opponent. He can throw himself into a fight as though it were the real thing, not a game. Once, at Tegernsee, he pursues me with such heat that he overlooks the high tension wires. His machine catches, hits the surface of the lake, and sinks. A replacement can no longer be obtained. I have to turn in my Fokker at once and am, again, grounded.

Through Angermund I have heard that the Rumpler Works want to institute air service between Munich and Vienna. I apply for a position as pilot.

It is a big thing. For the inaugural ceremony, the heads of the government have appeared on the "Oberwiesenfeld."† Silky toppers, rosy pates—and speeches, rolling across the field in full tones. There is picture taking, filming and much hand shaking. We are three pilots; Doldi, Basser, and me. The aircraft are old, converted military machines, not very comfortable, and weak in power.

Under way, we encounter a headwind. Only seven meters per second, but our "birds" can go against it only with difficulty. We are standing still. Finally, we all run out of gas and have to make emergency landings. None of us reaches Vienna on that day.

There, waiting on the airfield in Aspern, are the representatives of the city and high government agencies. In tails and top hats, they are waiting with speeches in their throats. They wait until evening, then go home disappointed.

† A large field used for public functions.

We are not over the city until next morning. We circle Stephen's Cathedral, and Doldi drops leaflets: "The first international air service Germany–Austria just opened with the landing of three commercial biplanes at Aspern."

But no one comes out. We land alone and unnoticed.

On the following day, we are to fly back. This time without ceremony. In front of the hangars stand a number of foreign officers, the Entente Commission. One of them approaches us and declares: "Your aircraft are confiscated. The import and export of aircraft is forbidden in Austria in accordance with the Treaty of St. Germain."

We protest and begin to reason with him excitedly. He turns his back on us. I want to get my goggles out of the cockpit but a small, yellow-faced man plants himself in front of me. I'm not even allowed to look in. The participants of the first international flight from Munich to Vienna return by train. The gentlemen of the Entente Commission are laughing. But, try as I might, I can't find any humor in this situation either.

An American has telephoned me at my home. Mr. William Pohl from Milwaukee. He is staying at the "Vier Jahreszeiten."‡ I am to meet him there in the evening for an important business discussion.

He is a typical American. He gets to the point at once. He wants to establish an aircraft factory in Germany. He wants to build a "Volks" aircraft that he expects to sell in large quantities on the other side. The name has already been decided upon. It's to be called "Everybody." He wants to know if I would like to be in on this.

"Yes I would, but I have no capital," I say reluctantly.

"Your knowledge, your connections, your name is what

‡ "Four Seasons."

we want; I'll put up the money," he says, as he waves me off. The firm is to be called Udet Flugzeugbau.§

The plan has been worked out in detail by the time we part, around midnight. We can start at once with the preliminaries. A shed is rented in Milbertshofen, and two workmen and an engineer are taken on. Building commences on the first model.

On July 15, 1921, a message arrives with a bang: "The Entente forbids any aircraft construction in Germany until further notice."

Pohl is back in Munich, and I meet him at his hotel. He shrugs his shoulders. "If you want to take the risk, it's all right with me."

Unauthorized building is prosecuted to the full extent of the law, with fines and imprisonment. I think for a moment. "Yes," I say.

Mr. Pohl is quite happy. "I expected nothing less from you," he replies.

I return to the shed and call the three-man crew together to explain the situation. "Things can go bad, boys," I finally concluded. "Where are the plans, Hiasl?" one asks the other. They don't make much of the chance they are about to take. They continue to work. Comrades . . .

But we have to be careful, very careful. I have the window panes painted blue, and the light inside is cryptlike. Bear traps are laid under the windows. A secret alarm bell announces anyone passing the garden gate.

One morning a worker comes to me. Yesterday, on his way home, he was accosted by a man. They went to have some beer, and the man paid for everything. He asked quite offhandedly what we make here. "Locks," said my man.

"Locks, why locks?"

§ Airplane factory.

"Locks for the mouth!" My man got up and left.

In the evening we see a man sneaking around the shed. "Is that him?" I ask, and the workman nods.

I ask the men to come around midnight. They understand without explanations.

Out in Ramersdorf, Scheuermann runs a factory for the manufacturing of beehives and chicken coops. I give him a call and ask if he is interested in breeding birds. Even on the telephone one must be careful. Scheuermann is a wartime buddy, a fighter pilot like myself.

"Come on out with your birds," he says.

About three in the morning a one-horse wagon rolls through the streets of Munich with our model, covered with a tarpaulin. I sit up front with the driver. The workmen hold the machine so it won't fall off. In haste, we could not mount it firmly.

In Scheuermann's chicken coops our bird is finally hatched. A few days before its completion, the building ban by the Entente is lifted. We can continue to work, out in the open.

May 12, 1922, is the big day. Pohl is there and a few workmen. The workers are wearing their Sunday best. The aircraft stands in front of the shed in festive decoration. Once more, the assembly is carefully gone over. The engineer stands close beside me. Suddenly, he pats himself on the forehead with the palm of his hand and runs into the design office. With rolled-up plans under his arm he emerges again and tugs at my sleeve and whispers with a pale face:

"An error . . . I can't understand how this could happen to me . . . the motor lies forty-seven centimeters too far back in the fuselage . . . I overlooked a comma in my calculations . . ."

Very quietly our bird returns to his nest. After four

days it reappears. The fuselage has been extended by the missing forty-seven centimeters. Thus a being has been created which, with its overlong rump, bears a likeness to a goose.

I climb in. The rpm counter is so far removed from the pilot's seat that I can't read the dial. The propeller is turned over; the bird winds itself into epileptic cramps but it finally takes off. The 30-hp Haake motor shakes the small crate so badly that I can't even recognize the ailerons. Everything vibrates as though the road in the air were paved with cobblestones. But I am flying—for the first time in two years.

The *Aero Club Aleman*¶ in Buenos Aires has invited me for an aerial meet. The Wilbur Cup is at stake.

We had consulted for some time. Pohl was against it; Scheuermann, now our technical director, was in favor. Udet Flugzeugbau has done well during the first year of its existence, and the growing pains of the first trails have been overcome. We have brought out the types U 2 and U 4 and sold them at a good profit. But a crossing to South America is expensive, especially in German money, and we are in the middle of the inflation. Finally, I go anyway. The possibilities of foreign trade are too enticing.

In Buenos Aires, Mr. Friedrich Blixstein comes aboard. The ship has been made fast along the pier. It is evening; the bight is filled with blue shadows, and the first lights are springing up in the city. Blixstein walks across the deck with open arms and grabs both my hands:

"My dear Mr. Udet, it is wonderful that you are here, that you really came." Small beads of perspiration are on his forehead.

¶ Spanish for "German Aero Club."

"Since you invited me . . ." My reserve in no way dampens his enthusiasm.

"Would you like to see how I prepared for your arrival?" He pulls a thick bundle of newspapers from his coat pocket and unfolds them with nervous fingers. *"As de los Ases"*** it says beneath my picture; the rest of the Spanish text I can't read.

We stroll up and down the promenade deck. Blixstein has hooked his arm under mine. I dislike this kind of familiarity, at least from men. But he has presented himself as the business manager of the Aero Club Aleman, and the Aero Club Aleman has invited me.

Walking along, he expounds on his plans. I will have to travel around the country with both machines. The Aero Club will, of course, pay the freight. I have been put up at the Plaza Hotel, "the best hotel in the city," says Mr. Blixstein. Then we drive to the hotel. A marvelous box, a cross between Romanesque pomp and American objectivity.

Blixstein accompanies me to dinner. He talks very much. Right after dinner I excuse myself: "I'm tired from the voyage." In my room, I stand by the open window for a while. The streets below are brimming with heat, noise, and lights. It is a strange feeling to look into the human flood of a strange city. "Will they trod you underfoot, or will you be the victor?" I ask myself.

Next morning I go to the office of the Aero Club Aleman. Blixstein had left me a card with its address. The car leaves the luxurious streets, the houses becoming smaller and more dilapidated. I finally reach a gray office complex, the quarters of the Aero Club Aleman.

There is only one secretary in the office. Blixstein, in shirt sleeves, walks up and down, dictating. He appears quite

** Spanish for "Ace of Aces."

businesslike. He shows me one of the circulars he had printed. The text on the right is in German, that on the left is in Spanish. With surprise I read: "Mr. Blixstein, general representative of Udet Flugzeugbau in Munich, has the honor . . ."

"Hm," I say with knitted brow, nothing more. But Blixstein has understood me anyway.

"I'm just dictating our contract," he declares, "the usual conditions. If you want, you can wait for it."

I'm not waiting. By myself, I walk through the hot, dusty streets back to the hotel. I must save money. My hope is the day of the Wilbur Cup Race. There I can show what our small machines can do. I'll have to hold out until then.

Eating is an art when one is short of cash. The eye skims along the price columns. This menu, when translated into marks, totals up to the weekly wage of a German worker. I decide on ravioli. It is the cheapest on the card. The waiter goes without batting an eyelash—a good hotel.

When I order ravioli again on the next day, he only gives a slight raise of the left eyebrow. "Stomach ailment," I mumble.

He bows deeply. Stomach ailments are elegant, empty wallets common.

It is late in July, and the heat sizzles in the streets. Only in the bar is it quiet and cool. I often sit there, sipping a cocktail and spooning the obligatory soft cheese. It stands on the table like a giant wheel, free, for the use of the guests. It makes one thirsty. But for me, it replaces supper. When the bartender looks my way I dreamily play with the cheese spoon.

The day of the Wilbur Cup Race is the ninth of August. It is a handicap race, more for the trade than the general public. The airfield is in the country outside the city, closed in with a wooden fence. Blixstein has come out with me. He takes me around, introducing me to sports writers and representatives of British and American firms. They are polite but reserved. Blixstein treats me like a son, with great expectations.

Then, the races begin. My little U 4 with the 55-hp Siemens motor is strongly handicapped. Spad, Curtiss, and Nieuport are represented by "birds" with powerful engines. But the U 4 stands up well. When it lands, I have the feeling that Udet Flugzeugbau has been well served by its workers. Blixstein says: "Wait for the press tomorrow, then we shall see. Our entire Argentinian business is dependent upon the critics' reactions."

Next morning, I have papers brought up by the hotel bellboys. There are reports on the Wilbur Cup Race in all of them. The U 4 is hardly mentioned.

I call up Blixstein at his office. He is quite short: "I'll come to your hotel this afternoon."

I stay in my room the entire day. Blixstein takes his time. He does not arrive until evening.

"Nice mess," he says as he walks in. "The Americans have the better connections with the press." He throws himself into an armchair with his legs thrown over the armrest.

"We'll have to change our method of operation. You will now do advertising flights for a cigarette firm."

"I don't do that kind of flying," I say with determination.

His face changes, and naked malevolence comes forth. "And how do you envision things to go on here?"

"I will fly," I say, "register at the air races in Rosario . . . perhaps we can sell one or the other machine."

He laughs. "May I point out to you that the bills of lading for your aircraft are made out to the *Aero Club Aleman?*"

"What do you mean to say?"

"The Aero Club Aleman has had twelve hundred gold pesos expenses in your behalf," he declares coolly. "Against the payment of this sum you can have these manifests; otherwise—you will just have to fly for the cigarette company."

As Blixstein leaves the tip of my toe itches. Rarely have I found a back so inviting.

I stroll into the bar for supper. There is cheese again. I am quite downcast. If I cabled to Munich for the money, they would probably send it to me. But in paper marks that's a lot of money. They might even be forced to curtail production to raise this sum. No, I must help myself.

A young man slides onto the bar stool next to me. He is blond, rosy, and tipsy. A Yankee. Probably arrived on the big liner this afternoon. We start up a conversation. He is a student from Boston, and this is his first big trip. He insists on treating me. We speak a mixture of English and French. "And what nationality are you?" he asks.

"German."

"Oh?" his face lengthens with surprise, "a Hun, who chops off the hands of infants?"

He slowly gets up and peels off his jacket. "I demand satisfaction," he says with a heavy tongue. He doesn't mention what for.

I have also slid off of my stool. He stands a head taller than I and seems to be in excellent physical condition. One can see the muscles ripple under his shirt sleeves. But my only salvation lies in a fast attack. I lunge at him and land a blow on his chin, so hard that the skin over my knuckles bursts. But he remains upright and looks around with surprise.

"Oh," he says, puts on his jacket again, sits down, and continues drinking. I wrap a handkerchief around my bruised knuckles and watch him out of the corner of my eye. But he doesn't make another move to attack me. Peaceful as a baby, he sops his twelfth cocktail.

A man with stiffly brushed-up hair taps me on the shoulder: "We would be pleased if you could come over and sit at our table."

They are Germans, countrymen.

"Blixstein?" says the man with the brush cut. "You weren't exactly lucky in your choice of partners, *Herr* Udet."

"I didn't pick him out." And I relate the scene that had taken place that afternoon. They are trying to figure out how they could help me.

"Tornquist," says one, "you must go and see Tornquist. He is an Argentinian of Swedish extraction, chief of the Argentinian railways and a sportsman through and through. He will certainly help you."

Next morning I'm in Tornquist's office. He has already been advised of my coming.

"We will salt Mr. Blixstein's ham," he says. He hands me a receipt for the two aircraft. "Your 'birds' had been guests of the Argentinian railways, *Herr* Udet."

For the last time I visit the Aero Club Aleman. As I come back down the stairs, my knuckles are bruised again. But this time I have placed my shot better.

Blixstein is gone, and now things should go well. I am a frequent guest of the German colony. In the Rosario air race, our pilot, Oliviero, in the U 4, flies the best time of the day. In the evening we celebrate the victory in the bar of the Plaza Hotel with German and Argentinian sportsmen. I meet the great racing driver Jorge Luro.

"If you don't have a better man," he says, "I would like to represent your firm in Argentina."

I nod, since I am unable to speak in pleased surprise. He pulls out his wallet. "I'll pay at once for one and one

half machines; the others will be taken care of on delivery."
He lays the bills on the table, and I casually rake them in.

A busboy puts cheese in front of me. I push it back.
"Curious, how one can shovel in so much cheese," I say with
grandiose flair.

I have left Udet Flugzeugbau, although the factory was a
going concern. The "Kolibri" has won the Rhoen Competition in 1924, and the "Flamingo" has made the grade as a
trainer. But then they start to build large aircraft. The Udet
"Kondor," a four-engine aircraft. I warned them, but they
wouldn't listen. So I left.

Angermund approaches me. "You know, actually you
could do some exhibition flying, like you used to do with
Greim back then."

I think this over for a long time. It is the only way to
continue flying, to stay in the air. "All right," I say, "if you
take over the arrangements."

And Angermund begins to work. He throws himself into
it with both his broad shoulders. He rents an office and begins
to assemble programs. He travels around the country and
negotiates with the cities.

Everything is arranged by the time I arrive. The areas are
cordoned off; ticket takers are hired. Angermund sees to it
that the curious are herded past the cashiers without being
able to take some other route.

I arrive and fly my program. In the beginning it's a lot of
fun. I chase balloons, roll turns, turn loops. The people ap-
plaud. But in time this too begins to get tiresome.

In the evening, when all is over, I go to pick up Angermund. He stands there like a sergeant in front of a company. The cashiers are lined up and unload their burden

of cash. He checks the figures and shovels the harvest into a laundry basket behind him.

"Come," I say, and we go somewhere to have a drink. Sometimes, Angermund tells of·what the people have to say. Some of it is droll. Once when I drove with a stalled motor, an enlightened female from Berlin declared: "You see, now he has run out of steam and he has to come down." And in Leipzig a Saxon flying enthusiast commented upon my loopings, flown close to the ground: "Ha, down here he's brave; he should go up high and try it!"

But most of the time we talk about the war. "Do you remember," says Angermund, "when crazy Franz shot you down? He sat there like a monument. And when he saw you, he shot your crate full of holes. I met him recently. He's a lawyer now."

This is the way we live. We stand in the present, fighting for a living. It isn't always easy. A lost engagement throws the monthly budget out of whack. But the thoughts wander back to the times when it was worthwhile to fight for your life.

FOUR MEN IN AFRICA

A young man with a heart for adventure has outfitted an expedition to East Africa. With aircraft and film cameras.

Four of us are sitting in an open tent. Schneeberger, the camera operator—a small, sinewy, and tenacious guy. During the war he had been the hero of Tofana. He had held the Schreckenstein, after it had been blown up by the enemy, with eight survivors out of thirty-eight. He doesn't talk much, but you can rely on what he says.

Then there is Suchocky and I. We are the two pilots of the expedition. The fourth, old Siedentopf, tells the famous story of the shot at Koettersheim.

Outside the tent is the African night. Jackals howl, the screeching laugh of the hyenas and the soft, low rustle of the treetops are all around us. Behind us is the surf of the sea. When one steps out of the tent, he can see the plains of Serengeti in the ghostly moonlight, smooth as the surface of a sea in calm weather.

Siedentopf is talking. From time to time, his shag pipe glows in the dark like a fireball, illuminating his lean, tanned face. Once he had been one of the richest men in German East Africa. He owned an entire crater with rich lava soil, full of game and water and as big as a German duchy. But he lost everything. Now he is the guide and consultant of our group.

"I could see," he says, "a peephole was being opened in the iron-clad door of the fort, a peephole like that in the curtain of a theater. We are three hundred meters off, under cover. 'Now you will see something,' I say to my boys, 'this target is Siedentopf's meat.' I take aim and squeeze the trigger.

The peephole closes, and the iron lid behind it falls. I have hit my man. He was . . ."

"The British commandant of Koettersheim," Schneeberger finishes for him, "and now we want to creep into our sleeping bags." Siedentopf gets up. "It's a cross I have to bear," he says sadly, "everybody knows the story of Koettersheim. From the Cape up to the Sudan. But I have told it to you only three times so far . . ."

We cruise over Serengeti every day. We always encounter game. Gigantic herds of gnus, fleeing from the strange "birds," groups of giraffe, lions in packs, mighty, thick-legged rhinos, charging after our shadow, angrily pushing their horns into the air.

It is blindingly bright, and we can see for hundreds of kilometers in the crystal clear air. But the work is hard just the same. From the aircraft the scene flies past too quickly for the camera to grasp. We have to skim close to the ground and against the wind with the motor throttled down. Only in this way can we obtain useful pictures.

On one flight we sight a group of lions, two males and three females. I fly six meters above them and photograph them with the stick between my legs.

The males lift their heads a few times and look up with suspicion, but the females have gotten up and eye the aircraft steadily, nervously whipping the ground with their tails. Suddenly one of them jumps up almost to my left wingtip. I am so surprised, I almost drop my camera.

Suchocky and Schneeberger are following in the second plane. They are flying quite low, at hardly three meters altitude. I turn around waving to warn them. Then it happens. Like lightning, the yellow body of the lioness streaks up. A swipe with the paw at the wing of Suchocky's machine and it lists, scrapes the ground, straightens up again, and goes on toward our tent, barely a meter above the ground. A long strip of silver material trails after it. The lioness, hit by the plane, is rolling in the sand. The other cats have risen and stare after us.

In camp we assess the damage. The front wing spar is broken; the rear spar and the aileron are cracked. The blow must have had considerable force. The claw marks can be clearly seen. There is also some hair and small blood spots. This is the only time I have seen an animal attack an airborne machine. Usually they attack only when we land and intrude into their domain.

We are flying over the valleys of the Esimingor, Suchocky and Siedentopf in their "Klemm," I alone in the little "Moth." Below us thorny brush and the dull green of the euphorbia woods. We want to land to shoot pictures. Suchocky glides down first, but just as he is about to touch down he pulls the machine up again. A round, flat stone lying on the ground has risen and charges after him—a rhino.

All this happens so fast I can hardly take it all in. Suchocky's machine wavers, hits a termite hill, and crashes to the ground. A dust cloud rises. The machine lies on its back, the broken undercarriage sticking up into the air.

I land close beside him. The rhino stomps around us in ever-narrowing circles. Two rifle shots send him off into the bushes, snorting.

"Suchocky, Siedentopf," I shout.

"Here," answers a pitiful voice. Suchocky must have been flung into the rear of the fuselage by the impact. It is too much for one man to right the "Klemm," so I haul out my bush knife and rip open the flank of the fuselage. Suchocky climbs out with effort and stretches out in the grass. The crackup seems to have shaken him badly.

I run around the aircraft looking for Siedentopf. There—a

brown hand—sticking out from under the fuselage, motionless. "Siedentopf," I shout, "Siedentopf," while I kick the fuselage with all my might.

Silence.

Endless seconds, then the voice of the old African: "Damned mess, stinks like the plague in this monkey cage."

After five minutes I am able to free him with my knife. I fly both of them back to camp. Suchocky has to lie down at once, but old Siedentopf appears for supper in the big tent. Bent and lame, he grumbles, but consumes enough corned beef for two.

Three months later—we have long since returned to Germany—I visit Suchocky in a Berlin hospital. He has a small face, like that of a ten-year-old child, and weighs eighty pounds. Shrinking of the liver, say the doctors. He shows me a letter from old Siedentopf. The old trooper has lost twenty-five pounds during the past several weeks; he has become a skeleton.

They both died almost on the same day.

I think that the spot on which they crashed was contaminated by cadavers. The doctors with whom I discussed this case shrugged their shoulders. They can't say what it was either. Suchocky and Siedentopf are out of it, but Schneeberger and I continue our work. We move our base to Babati, in the lands of the Ufiume tribe.

We start during the early afternoon and touch down forty-five minutes later. By car it would have been a ten-hour trip. We stop at the Figtree Hotel. We have noticed it from the air. Four small, round, straw-thatched huts, like beehives in the endless expanse of the prairie; close by, a flat, elongated building. A gigantic fig tree reaches out above it with its dark green branches.

Lord Lovelace has built this hotel in the middle of the prairie for motorists and fliers. One of the most memorable hotels I have ever stayed at. In each of the huts stand two clean beds, covered with white linen and hardly anything else. But in the main building is a bar that would do justice to any European luxury hotel. There is Martell, Hennessy, Meukov, and old Black and White.

We wriggle on the sugar crates at the bar and imbibe liquid civilization. The door is open. Through it one looks out upon the shaded yard and beyond to the horizon of the plains. A few Negro women walk past with earthen jugs on their heads. Slender bodies with a curiously gliding walk.

"I figure we'll have some good work here," says Schneeberger.

I nod.

The sky has been slowly closing in. On the way in we already noticed a thin curtain of clouds in the northeast. It grows and becomes a wall, and a blue shadow moves across the sweltering ground. It would be a good idea to get a roof over the "Moth."

We go out to the small airstrip where our aircraft stands. It has gotten quite dark, and the blue globe of the sky has become black. We grab the tarpaulin to pull it over the plane. At this moment, the sky is torn apart. A whirlwind descends, tears away our tarpaulin, and sweeps us and our aircraft along like wilted leaves. Then there is only water.

It is impossible to make out individual drops. The water comes down in a compact flood and broils around our feet. This may have lasted hardly a minute, before the deluge turns into an ordinary rain. In front of me, hardly fifty meters off, stands the last remains of the "Moth."

"Snowflea," I call in a wailing voice.

He appears from behind the wreckage. With his hair pasted to his face in streaks. He looks like a drowned rat.

The bartender had put away our glasses. "I thought you wouldn't be back," he says with a friendly smile. We ask for Martell, but this time in water glasses, for medicinal reasons, because we are shaking from the cold.

Should we capitulate, leave the dead "Moth" behind, and go home? Or should we try to patch up the old crate and give it another try? The Martell warms our stomachs like a stove. The storm has moved on, and the evening sun glares in the west, glistening on puddles and dew drops in the prairie grass and on the steam rising from the ground. We will continue to fly.

On the next day we drive to Aruscha. We pick up Baier, our mechanic with the main party, and bring along two German carpenters, Bauer and Bleich. They throw themselves into their new task with large glue pots and much zeal. They are busy for days. Snowflea hops around with the camera, photographing slim Babati girls, broad-chested and proud men, and loads of Negro children. "They are so nice," he says, "because you can't see the dirt on them."

But I have lots of time.

Curious people go in and out of Lord Lovelace's Figtree Hotel. Auto tourists mostly. Sometimes, dark characters on their way to the tribes in the south on dark business. More attractive are the local farmers. Whoever can live here in this solitude must be a whole man or he becomes a bum.

There is an American, tall and broad-shouldered, with a domed pate. He comes every two or three days, stops at the bar to toss down a few Black and Whites, pays, and leaves again. His name is Sullivan. The bartender tells me that Sullivan's wife ran off. She is supposed to have been quite beautiful. He is still waiting for her to return.

One evening we get into a conversation. We talk about cocoa beans, cotton plantations, and the new Empire tariffs. In the end he invites me to go on a buffalo hunt the next day. He picks me up in his car at dawn. We bump over the prairie so that the clumps of tree sway up and down like islands in a fog.

We stop near a small grove with a large rock in front. He points to its top. It's a natural shooting perch. He himself dives into the brush. He wants to supervise the drivers himself. I stay by myself. In front of me, the woods appear like a green wall. Behind me, the broad expanse of the prairie, wavering in the sun. It is quiet; only the cicadas chirp in the brown grass, and from a treetop sounds the disharmonious call of a bird. The drivers come on without any noise, so sensitive is the buffalo's hearing.

A rustle. The broad black head of a buffalo with broadly sweeping horns pushes his head through the curtain of foliage. He sniffs at the air and comes out into the open. It is an old, strong bull. A loner who lives out his last days away from the herd.

He is eighty meters off. I take aim and fire. He starts, turns clumsily, and trots off into the brush. Immediately after, Sullivan appears. He waves, and I run toward him. He points at the dark green leaves of a bush, spattered with bright red, foamy blood.

"Lung shot," he says appreciatively.

This time, I am to take a stand in a different location, thirty meters out in the open prairie. Sullivan returns to the drivers. This time I hear the buffalo long before I see him. Snorting and breathing hard, he breaks cover. Then he stands there, head lowered and his small, bloodshot eyes fixed on me. I give him the *coup de grâce,* and he collapses practically at the sound of the rifle. Slowly I stroll up to him. He lies there without motion. Blood is coming from his mouth and from a head wound. I look down at him. It is no great accomplishment to shoot a buffalo. The weapons are too unequal in such a fight.

The drivers come running out of the bush, shouting. Sullivan is among them.

"Wouldn't you like to be photographed with your kill?" he asks. I shake my head, "No." I understood the enthusiasm of his question, but I wouldn't have wanted to pose anyhow.

"That's good," he says. "I would have been disappointed if you were like the rest of them." He didn't say whom he meant by "the rest of them."

The black men fall upon the cadaver with long knifes, gutting it and cutting large chunks of meat from the quarters. A fire is lit, and the meat is roasted on the spit. Although it's a bit tough, it is tasty.

We drive across the prairie back to the Figtree Hotel. The sun is already in the west, a fiery balloon, bathing the entire landscape in a reddish haze.

"You can't imagine how they hunt here," begins Sullivan. "There are some characters who haven't hunted anything but dollars all their lives. From their ships, a secretary will send a telegram to the white hunter in Nairobi: 'Mr. Moneybags would like to shoot three lions, two buffalo, and an elephant. If possible, in three days.' The white hunter obtains the license from the British government and equips the expedition from the cook to the last cartridge. They call it a 'safari.' Then, off they go to the hunting grounds. The lion is already standing there, eating the zebra that has been thrown to him.

"The gentleman with the dollars shoots, and the lion keels over. 'Not even the Prince of Wales got one like that,' proclaims the white hunter and closes his eyes. Thus he hides himself from the hunter's stupid pride and the bare spots in simba's hide, whom the hunger of old age had driven to his doom.

"Then the man from the U.S.A. has himself photographed with his bag, usually with his foot on the lion's mane. If the white hunter is not yet hard-boiled, he is ashamed of himself, because he himself was once a hunter, but money has gotten the best of him. Now he sells himself as a guide for hunting expeditions. In doing so he gets rich and fat, has cars, a villa, and servants. But, in the process, real hunting has gone to the devil."

The sun has already disappeared behind the horizon, and the moon looks over the flatlands. Women are singing in the Babati villages. Schneeberger is already asleep when we return to the Figtree Hotel. We have a table set up outside in front of the house and drink.

"I knew one," says Sullivan. He drinks his whisky without soda in large, thirsty gulps. "That was a hunter! He came down here to hunt big game. He hired himself a white hunter because he had the money. The white hunter got him his lion. An old animal, peaceably gnawing away at his zebra cutlet. What does my man do when he sees him? He laughs, shoulders his gun, and declares: 'Cows I can shoot at home.'

"Shortly after, I met him here at the Figtree Hotel. He was a Canadian. Some guy. Flier, racing driver. Crashed a few times and sewn together like an old automobile inner tube. 'Life is a game of crap,' he says. 'It's enjoyable only on the borderline, where death begins.'

"He wanted to hunt with the natives, and I got him in touch with a Massai chief.

"Did you ever hear," asks Sullivan, "how these black men go after elephant?

"During the night, when the herd is asleep, one hunter, armed only with a short, broad-bladed bush knife, creeps into the brush where they spend the night. It has to be a moonless night, or they'll see him right away. He takes on the strongest bull, because of the ivory. He hacks his trunk off with a single blow and disappears in the brush. He has three seconds. If he isn't gone by the third second, the man will never be found.

"The maimed bull springs up, wild with pain, and crashes through the brush out into the open. Backward! Because an elephant without a trunk can't run forward any more. After fifteen hundred meters he collapses and bleeds to death. It is certainly beastly, but it is an honest fight, even Stephen. For ten dead elephants there is at least one dead man.

"The Canadian told me about it. He took part in one such hunt. He was with the Massai for four months, then he turned up again."

"Well?" I asked.

"He said it had been worth it."

They had met a lion. One of the loners. Such animals are as rare as great men. They never eat carrion, only young, fresh, and strong animals. They take the blood, some of the tender meat of the neck, and leave the remainder for the others. Their following always consists of a number of smaller lions. An entourage that feeds on the remainders of the royal feast. They had located such a lion and were trailing it. Fresh cadavers marked his travel route.

After a few days the Massai turned back. They were too far from their villages and wives. They wanted to go home. But the Canadian stayed on his trail. He tried every stratagem a hunter's brain can devise to bring the animal to bay. He staked out bleating young calfs while he himself sat high in a perch, tortured by mosquitos. He even hid in the belly of a gutted zebra. But the lion wouldn't come.

For days he followed the lion, becoming lean himself. Then he met his quarry. It was in a clearing. The lion stood there,

barely fifty meters away. He brought the gun to his cheek—
but he didn't fire. He simply couldn't.

Only a hunter can understand. He suddenly had the feeling
that this proud and royal animal stood closer to him than
many a human being. He brought his gun down and stood
there, staring at the lion. And the lion stared back at him
with his topaz yellow, sad eyes.

In the wilted prairie grass lining the clearing, the heads of
other lions appeared. The following was there, scenting a kill.
Suddenly, one of them shot out into the clearing, straight at
the man. The big lion turned his head. In three bounds he
was alongside the other; a blow of the paw into his neck, and
the smaller lion collapsed as if struck by lightning.

The Canadian returned to his bearers, walking slowly and
looking over his shoulder from time to time. But the lion
didn't follow.

"If someone else had told me this story," says Sullivan, "I
would have laughed. But I never heard an untruth from the
mouth of this man. By the way," he continues, "what happened can be deducted quite objectively. The young lion had
transgressed against the prerogatives of the stronger."

"I would like to meet your Canadian," I say.

Sullivan gets up. "Dead," he says. "Crashed while on a
flight down south. Burned up. They say there wasn't much
left."

The rainy season approaches, and the horizon is veiled in
gray. The main party of the expedition has already left Aruscha, driving to the coast in automobiles. Schneeberger and
I want to fly back. We take a reserve machine. A BFW "Moth"
has been patched together, but it is not usable for such a
long-distance flight. The day of our final start is like a carni-
val. The Babati girls hop about our machine with swaying

breasts, the bartender waves a white hat and Sullivan has come over from the farm. He is carrying a parcel wrapped in brown paper under his arm. It looks like a baby carriage. It is the horns of the buffalo I had shot with him several days ago.

"You are a hunter," he said, shaking my hand as though he wanted to tear off my arm. This is the greatest compliment he is capable of expressing while he is sober.

Then we fly off. The flat prairie disappears, and the three-thousand-meter peaks of the Mau Range reach up to us over the gigantic, blinking silver shield of Lake Victoria. From there, stretching north as far as the eye can see, the green sea of primeval forests. The foul, sweetish smell rises to meet us there.

Schneeberger is working, making backlighted pictures. Suddenly, a knocking, as though someone were rapping the aircraft from below with a hammer. I look forward and see that the reserve tank has come loose from its torn brackets. I look down. Treetops, crowning eighty-meter trees and no clearings, no villages. It is impossible to touch down. To the left are the waters of Lake Victoria. Near the shallow shores, crocodiles are floating lazily, like logs. They are quite clearly visible.

"Helmets off for prayer!" I think to myself.

Then, Schneeberger rises and throws his body forward, grasping the tank with both hands, and holds it down on its rest with the weight of his body, so that the feeder line to the carburetor won't break. If he can hold it until we reach Jinja, we will be safe. We are now skimming over the treetops. The pungent reek of the forest is hard to stand, but down here Schneeberger may be able to hold on longer than up where it's colder.

"Can you still hold on, 'Flea,'" I shout. The drone of the engine drowns my words. He doesn't answer, but his small, sinewy body appears as though it were molded to the tank.

In Jinja, the Ibis Hotel is a bit of European civilization flung into the African wilderness. We glide and land. I have to help Schneeberger out of the machine. He is stiff from the tremendous effort. He develops a fever during the night.

A Ford representative helps us to repair the damage. "Always stay with the highway through the Sudan," he says in parting, "just in case."

Above Lado we sight elephant herds. They are trotting through the high grass by the hundreds. The dust rises from them like clouds of steam.

A break in the fuel line. We have to land. There, a sandy spot, beautifully flat. It is good to be practiced in precision landing. The machine comes to a halt in barely fifty meters.

We are in the Sudan, close to the highway where a car passes once every week or two. The ground reflects oven temperatures, and there is no sheltering house near. We throw the tarpaulin over the plane and lie down underneath it. Schneeberger is feverish and moans for water.

I search around and find a spot where the grass is greener than elsewhere. This is where the moisture must be. I dig down and encounter some brackish sump water collecting in a brownish-yellow pool. I boil it in empty oil cans. It is involved work. I filter it through my pajamas, and Schneeberger drinks it in short, thirsty draughts. My production can hardly keep pace with his consumption.

Toward evening, a few natives come stalking around the tent. I wave at them, and they disappear. Finally, one of them comes closer. It is the son of the chief. Communication is difficult, but we finally determine that we have landed among the tribe of the Lau. They are familiar with aircraft and seem afraid and servile. However, once they realize that our "bird" is lame, their attitude changes at once. Somehow we are dependent upon them, and they let us know.

I ask for milk. After four hours he brings back our empty canteen and sticks out his hand. "Five shillings," he says. I shrug and offer him a cigarette case. It is of brass, made in Munich, but it shines like gold. He takes it and looks at it carefully and scratches at the button release. Yes, he is actually looking for the proof mark. Then he purses his lips in derision and hands it back to me.

"No gold," he says.

I don't even dare to offer him the glass beads I have.

We are stuck for two days. Schneeberger is doing badly, and the Lau tribesmen are getting more insolent by the hour. I have to stay with the tent constantly to prevent them from stealing. The heat is unbearable, the brain dehydrated. Slowly, a dull despair takes hold. A sick friend, no food, and the unfriendly natives.

Weeks can go by before a car shows up.

On the morning of the third day I hear a low hum from the distance . . . it grows into a roar . . . the song of an aircraft engine. Then it appears. It's a "Puss Moth." I pull the tarp away from Schneeberger and wave it, although the other pilot must already have noticed the bright silver of our bird.

The aircraft circles twice and lands. A slender, wiry man in khaki. "Campbell Black," he introduces himself. He brings us cigarettes and, above all, water, fresh drinking water. The Shell station in Juba, where we had last tanked, had telegraphed ahead, inquiring whether or not we had arrived. British generosity, British hospitality.

In the afternoon, a large military two-seater lands, bringing repair tools, gasoline, and an invitation from Wing Commander Sholto Douglas in Khartoum. The next evening we land there, and the colonel smilingly receives us.

"We were on the same front in 1917," he says, "and this makes for a bond, even when it was on the other side."

AMERICA ON THE WING

The sky vibrates to the sound of the engines. At least fifteen aircraft are in the air above the Cleveland airfield. Rolls, spins, loops, they're training for the meeting, to take place in three days. I land. The ground crews come running. Immediately behind them comes a man with horn-rimmed glasses and the starting roster.

"Colonel Udet from Germany?" he asks.

"Yes, Lieutenant Udet."

"You were reported to us as a colonel." He looks at me sternly.

"Sorry, I'm only a first lieutenant."

"Well, lets settle on major," he says, and tips his cap with his pencil.

A few gentlemen in plaid suits, reporters from the local press in Cleveland. They want to see the "Flamingo," the famous stunt plane. I point to the aircraft. "Here it is." They look at the machine and back at me. The Flamingo is now eight years old. It was the first of its type. In its youth it looked quite imposing. "Interesting," say the gentlemen from the press. They are courteous people and don't want to offend the foreign guest at the National Air Races.

I remain on the airfield for a while, watching the others practice. Sharp boys! With their heavy, powerfully engined aircraft they whizz through the air like projectiles. It'll be tough to hold up against such competition, I think. My sparrow with its 100-hp engine has to fly against falcons.

An aircraft races overhead and turns around the pylon. At the same moment a white gasoline trail appears, and dark smoke trails behind. The aircraft is on fire. The pilot reacts lightning quick, throws his machine on its back, pulls upward, and lets himself drop out of the cockpit. His chute opens at church steeple height, and he touches down barely fifty meters from me. I run toward him. He is standing there, brushing his brown corduroy trousers. Mechanics come running across the field.

"Accident," he states casually.

A man in mechanic's dress replies. "Thank God, it happened over the open field."

"O.K.," he says and brings out a cigarette and lights it. I observe him closely. The hand holding the match is steady. Unbelievably sharp guys, these Americans.

I look at the list of starters in the hotel. The Englishman Atcherley is here, the Pole Orlinsky, the Italian De Bernhardi. The best men, the best machines. And I am supposed to represent Germany in my 100-hp Flamingo. The peace treaty doesn't allow more horsepower for our machines.

I sleep poorly during the next few nights. To lose as an individual is easy. One competes, gives one's best. Victory or defeat are not in your own hands. But to lose for your country, this is bitter.

My Flamingo becomes somewhat of a celebrity in Cleveland, like a man who goes to a banquet in white tie and yellow shoes. And then the day of the National Air Races arrives. It is a bright day. We pilots of the foreign teams are picked up in cars, each in his own, accompanied by the howling sirens of the police escort.

Sky and people. From Cleveland, Chicago, and New York, from everywhere they have come. By train, by car, by plane. A national holiday in the air, these are the Cleveland National Air Races. It begins at nine in the morning and lasts into the night. Then the fireworks begin. Next day, the show continues. Every day for a week.

"One hundred thousand spectators," says a committee member and pulls his vest down over his stomach.

The contests begin. One program number after another, without letup. The heavy machines come hurtling out of the air in screaming dives, looping over the heads of the spectators and going straight up again. The army fliers come on like a swarm of hornets. A shout goes up from the crowd. Thirty bodies separate from thirty machines. Thirty parachutes open and descend like a white cloud.

"Major Udet, Germany!" drones the loudspeaker across the field as I climb into my crate.

Then I begin to work. I had laid out my program with care. It is clear that I can't compete with the strong machines of the others. They climb faster, roll with more agility, and do their loops and turns at a speed that would leave my Flamingo breathless. Thus I have attuned myself to slow flying, close to the ground—ground-floor aerobatics.

I fly upside down, close to the ground. I drag my left plane across the ground, raising a cloud of dust. I do loopings on a dead prop and pull the machine back up just a few meters in front of the grandstand. Finally I end up with a flat landing exactly on the spot from which I took off. Perhaps the others would have done as well had they sat in the light Flamingo. As it was, they had the heavy machines, I had the success.

As I land, the crowd jumps up from its seats, screaming, waving hats, arms, and scarves. A radio reporter grabs me and pushes me in front of a microphone. Colonel Rickenbacker, America's most successful ace with twenty-four* victories, is already standing there. A tall man with a lean, sharply cut face. Like a white Indian. We are elevated high above the heads of the crowd.

* Rickenbacker is officially credited with twenty-six victories.

"We met for the first time over Soissons," says Ricken-backer. His voice reverberates across the airfield. "There were seventy of us then. And when night fell, only fifty-two of us returned to our field. We fought many another fight, and other men fell. But we both stayed alive, and that's the best part of the whole thing, because we can now shake hands and show the American youth that honest enemies can become honest friends when the fighting is over."

Rickenbacker shakes hands with me, and the crowd breaks into a cheer. We stand on our pedestal like statues with iron faces.

Suddenly, Rickenbacker bends down to me, a grin on his lean face, and pats his hip pocket meaningfully: "Have a drink with me," he whispers. It is still the time of the great Prohibition over here. I nod back. Then we stand again like two statues, receiving the applause from the crowd.

At the Air Races, each nation has its special day of recognition. For "Germany Day," a special surprise has been prepared. After my exhibition flight I am supposed to meet Lieutenant Wanamaker. I had shot him down in July 1918.

Wanamaker comes, accompanied by his wife, toward me. He has obviously prepared for this moment.

"Hello, Ernest," he booms into the microphone, "have you ever put on weight!" This sounds easy, elegant, and straight off the cuff.

I produce a bit of canvas I had been holding behind my back. It is the serial number of his aircraft, in which I had shot him down back then. And suddenly, his well-prepared humor deserts him.

"That's real nice," he stammers—"really nice, that you would think of this." He has completely forgotten that we are standing in front of the microphone.

"You know what," he says, "when this whole business here

is over, come and visit us in Akron. My wife and I would be happy, wouldn't we, Mildred?"

Mrs. Wanamaker nods a bit embarrassedly. "Yes," she whispers. But the crowd starts cheering. The Wanamakers score a success. More so, probably, than he would have, had he completed his Wild West speech.

After the conclusion of the Air Races I drive across to Akron. The Wanamakers live in the green suburbs. A warm nest, full of middle-class comfort. In the evening we sit at a round table. Wanamaker has obtained some German wine in my honor. He pours me one glass after another. We talk about his job. He has become a State Attorney. We speak of the war. But the images of those days won't come alive again. Not until I am lying down in my room does it all come to life again.

It was on July 2, 1918, at dawn. Flak awakened me. It was quite near. I ran to the window. "Behrend," I shouted, "ready the machine!" He is already galloping across the field toward the hangar. I ran down in my pajamas. I slipped into my flying suit as I was running along. I took off and climbed to an altitude of three thousand meters. It was icy cold. The smoke puffs of the flak show the way. Two squadrons had bitten into each other. Eight Nieuports against seven Germans.

I recognized Loewenhardt's yellow Fokker pursuing an opponent. Another was getting onto his tail, and I had to crowd him off to protect Loewenhardt. Absorbed in the pursuit of his quarry, Loewenhardt had apparently been oblivious of the impending danger. But the American in front of me was equally oblivious. Slowly I let him slide into my sights. At the next moment the Nieuport took my burst in its engine.

With gasoline trailing, he dived, flattened out, and dived again and hit the ground with force. I landed near him. The pilot was creeping from the wreckage. I approached him and offered a cigarette. He thanked me and introduced himself: "Lieutenant Wanamaker," and pointed to his thigh with gritted teeth: "Broken."

The medics came and lifted him onto a stretcher. A field-gray soldier came by and shouted: "Three Americans have just been brought down!" Wanamaker asked me what he had said, and I interpreted: "Oh, a very good morning for us." That was the last I had heard of him.

Family pictures are hanging on the walls of the room. Group pictures and portraits; some of them are old-fashioned daguerreotypes. Had he died, I would have never come to this comfortable town. Then the woman with the blond hair would have hated me. Me, the one who killed her husband.

But it is good that there is a world of men beyond the warm light of the lamp. A world of contest, where the hate of the weak can't take root. "A very good morning for us, Lieutenant Wanamaker," I think as I turn off the light and go to sleep.

When I arrived in Hollywood, I was an unknown, at least when measured against the popularity of the movie stars. Three days later I am known to every insider. I am invited, handed around, interviewed.

A big man in the film industry had said after my first day of flying: "I will soon have to talk to this Major Udet." This is entirely sufficient to become well known—in Hollywood. Since then, I also circulate in the villas of the movie stars. They are mostly nice, simple, and industrious people. Most of them exhibit their eccentricities only for public relations purposes. Only one thing seems to be common to all of them— swimming pools.

Here they compete with hard-bitten ambition as to who possesses the largest and most comfortable basin. As far as I can

18. Bodenschatz, Udet, Bolle.

19. Goering,
Von Wedel,
Schulte-Frohlinde.

20. Back with the *staffel* on June 28, 1918, after bailing out.
On the right: Drekmann.

21. Goering, last C.O. of the Richthofen group.

To my dear friend
"Major Ernst Udet"
I am glad we are both
here to talk about the old days.
Eddie Rickenbacker 1931

22. Eddie Rickenbacker, the most successful surviving American fighter pilot.

23. René Fonck, the most successful surviving French fighter pilot.

24. William A. Bishop, the most successful surviving British ace.

To my gallant friend of the black cross with best regards

25. In Los Angeles, Roscoe Turner gives me the final aerial note from the student from Ontario.

26. U 4 of the Udet Aircraft Company in South America, 1923.

27. Landing on the Moenchjoch in Switzerland.

28. In the African interior.

29. Schneeberger and Suchocky examine the damage done by the lioness.

30. National Air Races in Los Angeles.

31. The foreign team in Cleveland: De Bernardi (Italy), Orlynsky (Poland), Al Williams (U.S.), Udet, Cubita (Czechoslovakia).

32. Arctic night.

33. Our expeditionary ship in Nugaitsiak.

see, Harold Lloyd's takes the cake. One can stroll on the bottom of his pool in a diver's helmet.

Mary Pickford is interested in aerobatics. We make a bet, and I win. With the wing plane of my Flamingo I pick her handkerchief off the ground.

Next morning a man visits me at my hotel. Did I already own an automobile here?

No.

Did I want one?

Perhaps, if it isn't too expensive.

It will cost nothing. The car is standing in front of the hotel. A four-seater limousine. If I pick a handkerchief off its roof with a wing, like yesterday with Mary Pickford, it will be mine.

The public relations manager of the auto manufacturer has brought his photographer along. Five minutes later I own a car.

I am in Hollywood for three weeks when I finally get "the word" from the movie man. The general manager has requested that I have a talk with him. He jumps into the matter with both feet. "We want to do a Richthofen film and need a flying consultant."

He names a sum. It's fantastic. I think for a moment. Richthofen? No! He's too big for Hollywood. "It's out of the question," I say.

The man shrugs his shoulders: "Too bad." But he doesn't press me, he doesn't inquire into my reasons for refusal. Objective. Unsentimental. American.

"Have a drink."

And we drink together.

The chairman raises his voice. He has a distinguished, two-pointed beard.

". . . and now we have a happy surprise for our flying hero. Among us is a man, a simple man, who saved Lieutenant Udet in a hail of enemy fire in 1918. *Herr* Mueller, please!"

Thumping cheers from the crowd.

A man climbs onto the podium, a little hesitant and embarrassed. I could swear that I have never seen this man before in my life.

"Now, *Herr* Mueller," encourages the chairman, "greet *Herr* Udet."

Mueller begins to talk in a dull, throaty voice and says quakingly: "It makes me happy to see you once again, Major."

I look him over from top to bottom. His cuffs are frayed, his shoes are in need of repair. In his protruding eyes, however, there is fear. The fear of one downtrodden by life, fighting for his last chance. "So give him a chance," I think and walk toward him.

"I thank you, *Herr* Mueller," I say in a loud voice and shake his hand. Thundering applause fills the hall. Mueller blushes, and suddenly he begins to talk in a resounding voice. He tells how he found me almost unconscious in the barbed wire. How he lifted me over his shoulder and carried me back under a hail of fire, like a mother carrying her child. When he finishes, the band has to play a flourish to quiet the crowd, so loud is the cheering and shouting. Down on the floor, Mueller is ringed by reporters. Once in a while he throws a shamefaced, smiling look up at me. Then he continues to answer questions.

A few days later I hear from a friend that Mueller has found employment in a slaughterhouse. He had been out of work for a long time. "Give him a chance," I think. An American motto—and a good one.

ON THE EDGE OF THE WORLD

David has shot a seal. He has pulled him onto the sand and begins dressing him. It is a lean animal, because we are in the early summer. The hot season has used up all his fat.

We sit on a bench in front of a small hut made from turf, watching David. Behind him the gray-green sea flows with only a light surf. Mighty icebergs are riding the waves, gliding by like gigantic swans. Only once in a while, one of them breaks up. Then thunder sounds through the fjord like artillery fire, is reflected back from the perpendicular basalt cliffs of the mainland, and continues to hover in erratic tones for some time after. The iceberg throws off its young, wallows around in the water, generating five-meter waves, which finally roll out in the surf on shore.

David has finished his work and is wiping his bloodied knife on his bear skin breeches. He walks ahead, and his wife follows him. She carries the kayak. Then come the children. Each packs a bundle of meat on its shoulders, as big as its thin arms can grasp. When David passes he greets us with measured ceremony. He is a great hunter. But his wife smiles at us so that her teeth glisten in her reddish-brown face.

Only the skeleton of the seal has remained behind in the sand, and the innards. Already the dogs have fallen upon them in a wriggling mass of hairy bodies so that it is difficult to recognize individual animals. Suddenly they scatter howling, forming a broad passage. Striding through it comes Nanunsiarssuit, the "bear hunter," the largest and strongest dog in the entire village, the king of all the dogs in Igdlorsuit.

The others have left the spoils and sit baying in a circle,

as though a man stood in their midst, swinging a seal whip, flailing the hide off them. But the "bear hunter" pays no attention to them. He sniffs at the skeleton and what little is left of the innards, lifts his hind leg, and sends a thick jet spraying down on these remainders. Then, with slow dignity, he walks through the circle of the other dogs. Again, a passage opens for him.

Schneeberger jumps up: "I must have that dog!" he says. Schriek and I look at each other over his head and smile. We have been in Igdlorsuit for six weeks. Long enough to know that David, the hunter, would rather part with his right hand than sell his Nanunsiarssuit.

In the north, a red flare climbs over the water, followed by two green ones. For a moment they stand at the apex of their rise like flaming skylarks; then they dip into the sea. Fanck's signal to start photographing. Schriek and Schneeberger are to join him. The two Eskimos in their rubber pants are already stamping through the village, down to the beach to ready Schriek's aircraft. Schneeberger and Schriek have gone into the house to put on their furs for the flight. They come out and take leave of me. Then I see their small "Klemm" disappear in the north. It dips along the basalt cliffs like a sea swallow.

It is sixty kilometers across the waters of the fjord and up to Nugaitsiak. Up there is the camp of the expedition. Fanck is there with the other members of the party. They are shooting the film *SOS Iceberg*. They need solid, packed ice to get near the icebergs.

Only Schriek, the mechanics, and myself have remained behind in Igdlorsuit, because this is where the only flat beach is to be found. And we need a sandy beach to bring our machines in.

Sometimes Schneeberger comes down for a visit. Together

we have filmed the Alpine movies *Piz Palu* and *Storms over Mont Blanc*. We were in Africa together. Such work makes for every bit as much of a bond as life in the trenches did.

In the beginning, working together was difficult. But, in time, we learned to communicate between the aircraft and the ground. Flares call us from the distance, and colored bars on Dr. Fanck's tent give us directions during the filming. Now we even have mail service to and from Nugaitsiak. The mail bags are suspended between two high poles. We catch them in flight and drop incoming mail down to them. We even have stamps. The American artist, Rockwell Kent, has designed and hand-printed them. He spends three-quarters of the year up here in Igdlorsuit. The Eskimos love him like an older brother because he possesses the wisdom of the disappointed, a love of nature, and a heart for simple people.

In the beginning, flying wasn't easy. Blue ice floats closely beneath the surface of the sea. Clear as glass, it is invisible from above. But, if one hits it with the floats during a landing, the bottom is gone. Although we have been here only a few weeks, Baier and Buchholz have already patched forty holes.

Once my motor failed and I had to set down on the water between two icebergs. Both were coming at each other with considerable speed and could have easily crushed me. I climbed out of the cabin onto the float and was able to turn over the prop. I just barely had time to grab the stick and get out from between the bluish, glistening, seventy-meter walls.

Schriek also had an accident. Only yesterday his fuel line broke. He had to come down in the open water. It took me four hours to tow him in at the end of a steel cable. We had a cross wind, and the sea was choppy.

Evenings, we sit on a bench in front of the small wooden

church, where we occupy the upper floor. Sometimes we play the harmonica. Then all the girls congregate around us in their colorful, fur-trimmed Sunday best. But mostly we are silent and we smoke. Then came old Daniel, David's father, who was himself a great hunter in his earlier days. He sits down next to us, spreads his crinkled hands in the pale sun, and chews whale blubber. It is cut into small dices and has a walnut flavor.

Daniel eyes our tobacco wistfully, but he never begs. He is much too proud. Sometimes we give him a swallow of whisky. Then he laughs and starts to talk. Rockwell Kent, sharing the bench with us, interprets. The old man tells us stories of the great hunts. He stands up and stretches, his arms akimbo. This is the way he says the polor bear came at him.

They were all alone, way up on the edge inland ice. The dogs were crouching in a circle, baying at the bear. One of them jumped up and at the white foe. The dog rolled in the snow with a broken spine. A second fell from the blow of a paw. A third.

Then Daniel took on the bear himself. He did so with a harpoon, because they did not yet possess firearms. With his old, shaky hands he grabs a paddle and waves it around in the air. He looks pathetic, but yet not ridiculous. Because here, a man is talking of his deeds of the past.

The bear grabbed the harpoon with his teeth and paws. It splintered like an icicle. This is when Daniel whipped the long knife out of his boot and went for the animal. He ducked the deadly embrace and rammed his knife into the bear's heart from below. Blood spurted out in a high arc above him . . . the blood of his deadly enemy. And the bear sank to the ground, and the dogs were all over him. Old Daniel coughs. He coughs so hard he has to lean against the boarding of the church. Then he spits into the sand. He is spitting blood.

He shakes his head, gives a small grin, and creeps back into his hut without a word of parting. He is consumptive and hasn't much time left. Many are consumptives up here. During the single Arctic summer we spent in Igdlorsuit, seven people die in the village. Seven out of seventy.

Three flares rise from the camp at Nugaitsiak. This means I should land. This isn't easy at this stony beach. Two men come to help me in, and I go up to the tents.

Everyone is excited. Dr. Sorge, the scientific adviser of the expedition, is missing. Eight days ago he had gone north in a paddle boat toward the Nink Glacier.

"You don't have to worry for seven days," he had said laughingly to his wife. "But if I don't return by the eighth, notify Fanck and the others."

Then he took off in his small Klepper collapsible boat, disappearing in the narrow channels winding through the pack ice. He went by himself, refusing the Eskimos who wanted to accompany him. Today is the eighth day, and during the morning a hunter had arrived who was up in the Kangerdluk Fjord, hunting seal. Close behind the big waterfalls he had found the wreckage of a collapsible boat on the pack ice. He brought back a piece of the stem. No doubt it is part of Sorge's boat.

Schneeberger and I take off at once. We fly up the Kangerdluk above the pack ice, between the nearly thousand-meters-high walls of the mountains that ring the gigantic basin of the inland ice. When we reach the waterfall, standing like a white marble column in the dark basalt, we cruise up and down.

From the cracks in the ice, the cold of the sea steams up

to us. Sometimes we see blue shadows on the glistening blue-white surface. But when we go down, it turns out to be only a block of ice, blackened by the earth. Gas is running short, and we have to return. As we land, the entire camp comes running toward us.

I go up to Sorge's tent. His wife is waiting there, sitting on the narrow cot. Leni Riefenstahl* is with her, with a sisterly arm laid over her shoulder. Gerda Sorge doesn't cry. She sits there silently with a stony face, clenching her hands so that the knuckles turn white. This desperate woman's hands are more terrible than tears.

I have the plane gassed up for a second start. This time I'll go alone. But Schneeberger is already climbing into the crate. "Four eyes can see better than two," he declares.

We fly. This time I want to go farther north. The thought comes to me that he had his accident much farther north and that the pack ice has brought the wreckage of the boat farther south. Our altitude is about midway between the bottoms and the tops of the cliffs. From time to time we have to swerve to avoid the peaks of icebergs, while the fjord is becoming narrower and darker.

The Nink Glacier—Sorge's objective—is a dome of shimmering ice, fifteen hundred meters wide. It rises like a glass green wall one hundred and twelve meters out of the sea. This is where the inland ice pushes into the sea with all its might. A look upward and there—from the dark rocks at the southern edge of the glacier—a thin column of smoke rises straight up into the sky.

A bank and we go straight toward it. Schneeberger points down with an outstretched arm. A few "larger than life" men are standing on the mountains like sentries. I fly toward

* A German actress.

them. They are rocks dressed with Sorge's clothes. His colored sweater, his cap. They are to point the way to him.

Then we see him. The lean, full-bearded man hops around the fire, waving his arms like a priest of Baal. We circle and wave. With the stick between my knees I scribble a note. "In two hours, boat will be with you." I stick the note into an empty cartridge and throw it down. We watch him pick it up, then we turn back.

On the way we meet our motor boat, slowly pushing its way northward through the pack ice. Again we throw a note, advising of Sorge's position. In the camp there is happy excitement. We scrape together every last drop of gasoline for a third flight, because we are not certain that the boat can reach him today.

This time, Schneeberger cannot come along. On the observer's seat, tied together with a rope, is a large bag with food, fuel, and blankets.

Sorge has heard me coming. He stands on a peak and waves at me. Closely above him I circle, grab the bag, and lift it out of the observer's seat. Suddenly, I feel a sharp tug at my throat, and my head is pulled back and bangs against the back of my seat. The rope of the bag has caught around my neck and is choking me. The plane flits close to the ground. I grab my knife—a quick cut—and I'm free.

I grab the stick again and look down. The bag has landed in front of Sorge's feet. He hasn't noticed a thing and waves his clasped hands at me.

Six days later, Sorge is back in Nugaitsiak. He has experienced the mightiest spectacle a man has ever witnessed. The foaling of the Nink Glacier. Masses of ice, as large as all the houses of Berlin put together, have crashed into the sea. Water fountains rose three hundred meters. One of the tidal waves had carried off his boat, beached four meters above the beach level, and carried the smashed wreckage south.

In the afternoon we held a shooting match. I organized a rifle meet and put my Winchester up as a prize for the best marksman. All the men from Igdlorsuit were invited. And all came, with their firearms. Really old rifles, even a muzzle loader, was among them.

I am not a bad shot. During the shoots with the Richthofen group I had always held my own. But I couldn't keep up with the Greenlanders. They load awkwardly and carefully. But they stand like blocks of basalt and their hands are quiet, as though they were hewn of stone. Almost every shot is in the inner three rings; every other shot is a bull's-eye.

The winner of the meet and the Winchester is Imerarsuk, the "little watersack." He hugs it to him, strokes it, and runs laughing into his hut.

In the evening, David comes to me. His father, Daniel, is dying. He has one wish. He would like to fly over the fjord and Igdlorsuit in the "man bird."

"All right," I say. "Call the guys with the rubber pants so that they can get out the machine, and bring your father down to the beach."

Two carry the old man and lift him into the plane. I put the flying cap on him and fix his goggles. He is laughing like a child. We take off. The "bird" lifts off with effort, and we begin to spiral upward.

The sea is beneath us, yellow in the light of the fading sun. White icebergs are sailing on its surface. The year is already far gone, and winter is harnessing its black horses. Soon comes the night, the long night.

Higher and higher we fly. The earth huts of Igdlorsuit are as small as molehills; the church bashfully points its finger into the air. The mountains sink below, and the view is opened to the north, where the inland ice stretches endlessly to the horizon like a shield of steel.

Wonderful, the way the old man lives each motion of the aircraft, how he leans his body into every curve. The hunter who felt the motion of the waves in his kayak understands the laws of the elements.

The motor drones, and land and sea sink silently beneath us. Then a human voice sounds with full-breasted tones, in drawn-out, mightily booming notes. Old Daniel is singing.

He is still singing when we land, when they lift him from the boat and carry him into his hut. He sings until he disappears in its dark hollow.

Next morning, David is at my door: "My father died during the night."

I shake hands with him.

"You are my friend," he says, "you can always stay with me."

But I must go on. Soon the long arctic night will fall, and all life will come to a halt.

CURTAIN

My generation was formed by the war. It hit us during the decisive years. The weak were broken by it. In them, nothing but a paralyzing terror remained. In us others—and I am speaking of virtually all front-line soldiers—the will to live had become stronger and harder. A new will to live, which recognizes that the life of one counts for nothing, but that the life and the future of the society are everything.

For fourteen years we carried this knowledge with us through an alien world. They understood nothing of the greatness of our belief. They would hear nothing of the hard virtues of the soldier, loyalty, sense of duty, and the spirit of the last sacrifice. We were strangers among them and worked for our bread. I flew to live. But at the same time I had the hope that the idea of German aviation could be kept alive. I was on foreign continents. Everywhere I looked for fellowship. I searched and I found it in Germany, in America, in the African bush, and in Greenland's ice:

The fellowship of fliers! . . .

But secretly, we longed to see the spirit that formed us to work as an active force among the people to whom we are tied by the innermost bonds. This has happened, and this is why I am closing this book. Because my own life has become unimportant; it has immersed itself in the mainstream of our common German destiny.

We had been soldiers without colors. We have unfurled them once again. The *Fuehrer* has given them back to us. For old soldiers, life is worth living again.*

* It is not known whether this part of the book was written by Udet or by his Nazi masters. At any rate, he was made a scapegoat and forced to commit suicide by his old "buddy" and "last leader" the 1914–18 Richthofen Geschwader, Hermann Goering, who had become the chief of the World War II Nazi Luftwaffe. Unfortunately, for "old soldier" Udet, "life" was *not* "worth living again."

Appendix

VICTORY ROSTER OF ERNST UDET

DATE	TIME	AIRCRAFT DOWNED	LOCATION	VICTORY

Single-Seater Combat Command Habsheim

DATE	TIME	AIRCRAFT DOWNED	LOCATION	VICTORY
18/ 3/16	1710	Farman	Muelhausen	1

Jagdstaffel 15

DATE	TIME	AIRCRAFT DOWNED	LOCATION	VICTORY
12/10/16	1530	Breguet Michelin	Ruestenhart	2
24/12/16	1100	Caudron	Oberaspach	3
20/ 2/17	noon	Nieuport	Aspach	4
24/ 4/17	1930	Nieuport	Chavignon	5
5/ 5/17	1930	Spad	Bois d'Viller	6

Jagdstaffel 37

DATE	TIME	AIRCRAFT DOWNED	LOCATION	VICTORY
14/ 8/17	2030	Bristol	Lens	7
15/ 8/17	1025	Sopwith two-seater	Pont à Vendin	8
21/ 8/17	0845	De Havilland 4	Ascq, S. of Lille	9
17/ 9/17	0730	De Havilland 5	Izel	10
24/ 9/17	1220	British Pusher	Loos	11
28/ 9/17	1800	Sopwith Camel	W. of Wingles	12
28/ 9/17	1800	Sopwith Camel	W. of Wingles	13
18/10/17	1035	Sopwith Camel	Deulemont	14
28/11/17	1340	De Havilland 5	Paschendale-Poelcapelle	15
5/12/17	1430	S.E. 5	Westrosebeke-Poelcapelle	16
6/ 1/18	1615	Nieuport	Bixschote	17
28/ 1/18	1655	Sopwith	Bixschote	18
29/ 1/18	1200	Bristol single-seater	Zillebeke	19
18/ 2/18	1050	Sopwith Camel	Zandvoorde	20

Jagdstaffel 11

DATE	TIME	AIRCRAFT DOWNED	LOCATION	VICTORY
27/ 3/18	1150	R.E. 8	Albert	21
28/ 3/18	0910	Sopwith Camel	Albert Bapaume	22
6/ 4/18	1415	Sopwith Camel	Hamel	23

VICTORY ROSTER OF JAGDSTAFFEL 4 UNDER THE COMMAND OF OBERLEUTNANT UDET

DATE	TIME	VICTOR	AIRCRAFT DOWNED	LOCATION	VICTORY SQUADRON	UDET
20/5/18	1125	Lt. v. Rautter	Bristol	Warfusee	1	
27/5/18	1815	Lt. v. Rautter	Breguet	Pont Arcy	2	
31/5/18	1200	Lt. v. Rautter	Breguet	S.W. of Soissons	3	
31/5/18	1300	Lt. Udet	Breguet	S.W. of Soissons	4	24
2/6/18	1150	Lt. Udet	Breguet	N.W. of Neuilly	5	25
2/6/18	1820	Lt. Maushacke	Breguet	Montigny Labier	6	
4/6/18	1845	Lt. Drekmann	Spad	Longpont	7	
5/6/18	1200	Lt. Udet	Spad	S. of Buczany	8	26
6/6/18	1140	Lt. Udet	Spad	S. of Faverolles	9	27
7/6/18	1900	Lt. Udet	Spad	E. of Villers Cotterets	10	28
13/6/18	1745	Lt. Udet	Spad	N.E. of Faverolles	11	29
13/6/18	1745	Lt. Drekmann	Spad	N. of Noroy	12	
14/6/18	2000	Lt. Udet	Spad	N. of S. Pierre Aigle	13	30
23/6/18	1210	Lt. Udet	Breguet	La Ferte Milon	14	31
23/6/18	2015	Lt. Udet	Breguet	Area of Crouy	15	32
24/6/18	1000	Lt. Udet	Breguet	S.E. of Montigny	16	33
25/6/18	1845	Lt. Udet	Spad	Woods N. of Longpont	17	34
25/6/18	1845	Lt. Udet	Spad	Chavigny Ferme	18	35
27/6/18	2000	Lt. Drekmann	Balloon	Villers Cotterets	19	
28/6/18	0945	Lt. Drekmann	Spad	Puisseux	20	
28/6/18	0945	Lt. Maushacke	Spad	E. of Biercy	21	

DATE	TIME	VICTOR	AIRCRAFT DOWNED	LOCATION	VICTORY SQUADRON	VICTORY UDET
28/6/18	0950	Lt. Meyer	Spad	Villers Cotterets	22	
30/6/18	2000	Lt. Udet	Spad	Faverolles	23	36
1/7/18	1145	Lt. Udet	Breguet	Pierrefont-Mortefontaine	24	37
1/7/18	2055	Lt. Udet	Spad	E. of Faverolles	25	38
2/7/18	0815	Lt. Udet	Nieuport	Bezu St. Germain	26	39
3/7/18	0820	Lt. Drekmann	Breguet	Nouvron	27	
3/7/18	0825	Lt. Udet	Spad	E. of Laversine	28	40
3/7/18	2025	Lt. Drekmann	Spad	N.W. of Dompierre	29	
15/7/18	1640	Lt. Meyer	Spad	N. of Fossoy	30	
17/7/18	1045	Lt. Maushacke	Breguet	Dormans n. Vincelles	31	
17/7/18	1050	Lt. Koepsch	Breguet	Combizy	32	
18/7/18	0915	Lt. Maushacke	D.H. 9	S.W. of Authenay	33	
18/7/18	0930	Lt. Meyer	Sopwith Camel	Marauill	34	
19/7/18	1530	Lt. Maushacke	Spad	Hartennes	35	
20/7/18	2025	Lt. Drekmann	D.H. 9	Morsain	36	
22/7/18	1910	Lt. Koepsch	D.H. 9	S. of Braisne	37	
25/7/18	1930	Lt. Drekmann	Spad	Qulchy	38	
30/7/18	1830	Lt. Drekmann	Spad	N. of Grand Rozoy	39	
1/8/18	0930	Lt. Udet	Nieuport	N.E. of Cramaille	40	41
1/8/18	0930	Lt. Koepsch	Nieuport	S. of Braisne	41	
1/8/18	0930	Lt. Jessen	Nieuport	Cuiry House	42	
1/8/18	1215	Lt. Udet	Breguet	N. of Muret Crouttes	43	42
1/8/18	2030	Lt. Udet	Spad	N. of Baugneux	44	43
4/8/18	2005	Lt. Udet	Spad	S. of Braisne	45	44
4/8/18	2005	Lt. Jessen	Spad	N. of Vauxtin	46	

DATE	TIME	VICTOR	AIRCRAFT DOWNED	LOCATION	VICTORY SQUADRON	VICTORY UDET
8/8/18	1730	Lt. Udet	S.E. 5	Fontaine le Cappy	47	45
8/8/18	1830	Lt. Udet	S.E. 5	S.E. of Barleux	48	46
8/8/18	2040	Lt. Udet	Sopwith Camel	S.E. of Foucaucourt	49	47
9/8/18	1625	Lt. Udet	Sopwith Camel	S. of Vauvillers	50	48
9/8/18	2120	Lt. Udet	Sopwith Camel	S.E. of Herleville	51	49
10/8/18	1130	Lt. Udet	Sopwith Camel	S. of Marcourt	52	50
10/8/18	1600	Lt. Maushacke	R.E. 8	S. of Vauvillers	53	
10/8/18	1945	Lt. Udet	Sopwith Camel	S. of Fay	54	51
11/8/18	1000	Lt. Udet	D.H. 12	Chaulnes	55	52
12/8/18	1130	Lt. Udet	S.E. 5	Near Peronne	56	53
13/8/18	1945	Lt. Koepsch	Breguet	Bilancourt	57	
14/8/18	1900	Lt. Udet	Bristol Fighter	S. of Vermandovillers	58	54
15/8/18	1715	Lt. Udet	Sopwith Camel	Herleville	59	55
16/8/18	1040	Lt. Udet	Spad	S. of Foucaucourt	60	56
21/8/18	1830	Lt. Udet	S.E. 5	S. of Hebuterne	61	57
21/8/18	1915	Lt. Udet	Sopwith Dolphin	S. of Courcelles	62	58
22/8/18	0830	Lt. Udet	Sopwith Camel	N. of Braie	63	59
22/8/18	1230	Lt. Udet	S.E. 5	W. of Marcourt	64	60
31/8/18	1620	Lt. Koepsch	S.E. 5	Near Combles	65	
5/9/18	1915	Lt. Koepsch	S.E. 5	Paillencourt	66	
6/9/18	1055	Lt. Maushacke	Sopwith Camel	S.E. of Aubensheulle	67	
26/9/18	1620	Lt. v. Gluczewski	D.H. 9	S.E. of Kemnat	68	
26/9/18	1710	Lt. Udet	D.H. 9	Near Monteningen	69	61
26/9/18	1715	Lt. Kraut	D.H. 9	Buch	70	
26/9/18	1720	Lt. Udet	D.H. 9	S. of Metz	71	62

UDET'S LAST COMBAT REPORT

Jagdgeschwader
Frhr. v. Richthofen № 1.
Jagdstaffel 4.

Flughafen, am 29.9.18.

Luftkampfbericht.

1. Zeit (Tag, Stunde und Minute): 26.9.18   5,20 Uhr nachm.

2. Ort (Absturz oder Landestelle des Gegners): südl.Metz,   diesseits.

3. Flugzeugart: D. H. 9.

4. Besondere Kennzeichen und Staatsangehoerigkeit des Gegners:

5. Besondere Kennzeichen des eigenen Flugzeugs: Fokk.D.VII.4253.
   Rumpf rot, an den beiden Rumpfseiten Buchstaben " LO "

6. Namen und Schicksal der Insassen des feindlichen Flugzeugs: tot.

7. Hergang des Luftkampfes: Nach Abschuss des ersten D.H.9 griff ich das
Geschwader,das nur noch aus 5 oder 4 Einheiten bestand und sich
auf dem Rückflug befand, erneut an. Ich schoss den mittleren D.H.9
erst stinkend und sofort darauf brennend. Der Brand liess teilwei-
se nach und fachte wieder auf. Der Absturz erfolgte in Gegend südl.
Metz

Udet

Oblt. u.Führer

Zeugen des Luftkampfes:

Oblt.Göring,Jagdgeschw.Frhr.v.Richthofen
  "   v.Wedel, Jagdstaffel 11
  "   Frhr. v.Boenigk,Jagdgeschwader II.
Lt.d.R.Ioepsch, Jagdstaffel 4
  "   v.Radzack,
Flugmelde-Offizier Flakgrube 39. ....

An   Jagdgeschwader Frhr.von Richthofen No.1

Vorstehenden Bericht des Oblt.d.R. U d e t mit der Bitte
überreicht, die Anerkennung des Abschusses als 62.Luftsieg,185.Sieg der
Jagdstaffel 4 höheren Orts erwirken zu wollen.

Udet

Oberlt.d.R. und Führer.

(*Translation of Udet's Last Combat Report*)

Fighter Group
Frhr. v. Richthofen No. 1
Fighter Squadron 4

AERIAL COMBAT REPORT

1. *Time* (*day, hour, minute*): 26.9.18   5:20 P.M.
2. *Place* (*enemy crash or landing site*): South of Metz, our side
3. *Type of Aircraft:* D.H. 9
4. *Special Distinguishing Features and Nationality of Opponent:*
5. *Special Distinguishing Features of Own Aircraft:*
   Red fuselage, on both sides the letters "LO."
6. *Name and Fate of the Occupants of Enemy a/c:* Dead.
7. *Course of the Action:* After bringing down the first D.H. 9, I renewed my attack on the enemy formation, which now consisted only of four or five units and was on its return flight. I fired on the center D.H. 9 which, at first, began to smoke and then to burn immediately afterward. The fire died down and then flared up again. The crash took place in the area south of metz.

Udet

1st Lt. and C.O.

Witness of the Combat:

1st Lt. Goering, Fighter Group Frhr. v. Richthofen
1st Lt. v. Wedel, Fighter Squadron 11
1st Lt. Frhr. v. Boenigk, Fighter Group II
Lt. (Res.) Koepsch, Fighter Squadron 4
Lt. v. Radzack, Air Obs. Off., AA Group 39
          To
          Fighter Group Frhr. v. Richthofen No. 1
The above report of 1st Lt. (Res.) Udet is submitted with the request that it be forwarded to higher headquarters for confirmation as 62nd victory, 185th victory of Fighter Squadron 4.

Udet

1st Lt. (Res.) and C.O.

THE WITNESSES REPORTS OF
UDETS' LAST VICTORY

Jagdgeschwader
Frhr. v. Richthofen N⁰1.
Jagdstaffel 4.   Abschrift der Zeugenberichte zum Abschuss eines

D.H.9 am 26.9.18.

26.9.18.

Ich beobachtete gegen 5,15 Uhr wie die rote Maschine des
Oblt. U d e t erst einen D.H.9 abmontierend und kurz
darauf einen zweiten D.H.2 brennend zum Absturz brachte.
Gegend südöstl. Metz.

gez. Göring, Kdr.
des Jagdgeschw.Frhr.von Richthofen.

Ich beobachtete wie am 26.9.18 gegen 5,10 nachm. die hell-
rote Maschine des Oblt. U d e t zuerst westl.Metz einen
D.H.9 abschoss; er ging herunter und montierte ab. Oblt.
U d e t griff dann das fdl.Geschwader von neuem an,worauf
ein D.H.9 brennend südöstl. Metz abstürzte.

gez. v.Wedel,Oblt.
Jagdstaffel 11.

Ich sah vom Flugplatz Tidémont mit Scheerenfernrohr am
26.9.18 gegen 5,15 abends, wie ein roter Fokker innerhalb ei-
niger Minuten 1 D.H.9 brennend und 1 D.H.9 abmontierend abschoss.

26.9.18

gez.Frhr.v.Boenigk,Oblt.
Kdr.d.Jagdgeschwaders II.

Ich sah vom Boden aus, wie Oblt. U d e t ein Bombengeschwa-
der angriff und 2 D.H.9 abschoss. Die rote Maschine war vom
Boden gut zu erkennen, desgl.auch das Schiessen.Oblt. Udet
war auf ganz dichte Entfernung heran. Der erste zerplatzte
beim Anflug, der zweite brannte beim Rückflug.Zeit: gegen
5,00 Uhr.
26.9.18.

gez. Koepsch. Lt.d.R.
Jagdstaffel 4.

Am 26.9. 5,00 nachm.griff die rote Maschine einen D.H.9 an,
der sich rechts hinten am Geschwader befand. Der D.H.9 kippte
senkrecht, fing sich nach 200 m, überschlug sich und montierte in Gegend Monteningen ab.Darauf griff die rote Maschine
das Geschwader von vorne an und schoss einen brennend.

gez. v.Radzack,Leutnant.

Am 26.9.18 nachmittags 5,10 sah ich, wie Oblt. U d e t aus
einem engl.Bombengeschwader einen D.H.9 aus nächster Nähe angriff und beschoss, worauf das fdl.Flugzeug steil herabfiel
und abmontierte, die Trümmer fielen in Gegend Mühlen.

gez. Bender, Lt.d.R.
Jagdstaffel 4.

Wir griffen gestern abend 5,10 Uhr ein fdl.Bombengeschwader
auf dem Anflug nach Metz an. Ich sah, wie Oblt.Udet, der als
Erster heran war, einen D.H.9 angriff. Der Gegner kippte
nach wenigen Schüssen seitwärts und flog stinkend in der Rücken-
lage schräg abwärts. Der Beobachter stürzte heraus. Nach wenigen
Augenblicken zerplatzte der D.H.9.

gez. Kraut, Lt.d.R.
Jagdstaffel 4.

*(Translation of the Witnesses Reports of
Udet's Last Victory)*

26.9.18

Around 5:15 I observed the red aircraft of Lt. Udet first disintegrate a D.H. 9 and shortly thereafter bring a second D.H. 2* down in flames. Area southeast of Metz.

(signed) Goering, C.O.
Fighter Group Frhr. v. Richthofen

On 26.9.18, around 5:10 P.M., I observed the bright red machine of Lt. Udet first bring down a D.H. 9; it came down and disintegrated. Lt. Udet then attacked the enemy formation again, whereupon a D.H. 9 came down in flames southeast of Metz.

(signed) von Wedel
Fighter Squadron 11

From the Tidémont airfield I observed, through stereoscopic binoculars, a red Fokker as, at approximately 5:15 P.M. on 26.9.18, it brought down in a matter of minutes one D.H. 9 in flames, and one D.H. 9 disintegrating.

(signed) Frhr. v. Boenigk, 1st Lt.
C.O., Fighter Group II

From the ground, I saw Lt. Udet attack a bomber formation and shoot down two D.H. 9's. The red aircraft was easily recognizable from the ground, as was the shooting. Lt. Udet had closed to a very short distance. The first disintegrated during the approach, the second burned on the return. Time: approximately 5:00. 26.9.18

(signed) Koepsch, Lt. (Res.)
Fighter Squadron 4

On 26.9.18, 5:00 P.M., the red machine attacked a D.H. 9, positioned to the right rear of the formation. The D.H. 9 went down vertically, recovered after two hundred meters, overturned, and disintegrated into the area of Monteningen. Thereafter the red

---

* Although the original report said "D.H. 2," Goering obviously meant "D.H. 9." It was probably a typographical error.

machine attacked the formation from the front and flamed one.

(signed) v. Radzack, Lieutenant

On 26.9.18, 5:10 P.M., I observed Lt. Udet attacking a British bomber formation, bringing a D.H. 9 down from a very close distance. The aircraft fell vertically and disintegrated. The wreckage fell in the area of Muehlen.

(signed) Bender, Lt. (Res.)
Fighter Squadron 4

Yesterday evening toward 5:10 P.M., we attacked an enemy bomber formation flying toward Metz. I saw Lt. Udet, the first to reach the enemy, attack a D.H. 9. After a few rounds, the enemy turned on its side and fell obliquely in an upside-down position and smoking. The observer fell out. After a few moments the D.H. 9 crashed.

(signed) Kraut, Lt. (Res.)
Fighter Squadron 4

LEADING GERMAN ACES, 1914–18

Heading the list of more than three hundred German aces was Rittmeister Manfred von Richthofen, also known as the "Red Baron" because of his all-red Albatros and Fokker fighters. He was leader of the famous "Flying Circus" and was the ranking ace of both sides—friend and foe—in the First World War.

	Victories
Rittmeister Manfred *Frhr.* v. Richthofen	80
Oberleutnant Ernst Udet	62
Oberleutnant Erich Loewenhardt	53
Leutnant Werner Voss	48
Leutnant Fritz Rumey	45
Hauptmann Rudolph Berthold	44
Leutnant Paul Bäumer	43
Leutnant Josef Jacobs	41
Hauptmann Bruno Loerzer	41
Hauptmann Oswald Boelcke	40
Leutnant Franz Büchner	40
Oberleutnant Lothar *Frhr.* von Richthofen	40
Leutnant Karl Menckhoff	39
Leutnant Heinrich Gontermann	39
Leutnant Max Müller	36
Leutnant Julius Buckler	35
Leutnant Gustav Doerr	35
Hauptmann Eduard Ritter von Schleich	35
Leutnant Josef Veltjens	34
Leutnant Otto Koennecke	33
Oberleutnant Kurt Wolff	33
Leutnant Heinrich Bongartz	33
Leutnant Theo Osterkamp	32
Leutnant Emil Thuy	32
Leutnant Paul Billik	31
Rittmeister Karl Bolle	31
Oberleutnant Gotthard Sachsenberg	31

	Victories
Leutnant Karl Allmenroeder	30
Leutnant Karl Degelow	30
Leutnant Heinrich Kroll	30
Leutnant Josef Mai	30
Leutnant Ulrich Neckel	30
Leutnant Karl Schaefer	30
Leutnant Hermann Frommerz	29
Leutnant Walter von Bülow	28
Leutnant Walter Blume	28
Oberleutnant Fritz Ritter von Röth	28
Oberleutnant Fritz Bernert	27
Vizefeldwebel Otto Fruhner	27
Leutnant Hans Kirschstein	27
Leutnant Karl Thom	27
Hauptmann Adolf Ritter von Tutschek	27
Leutnant Kurt Wüsthoff	27
Oberleutnant Harald Auffahrt	26
Oberleutnant Oscar *Frhr.* von Boenigk	26
Oberleutnant Eduard Dostler	26
Leutnant Arthur Laumann	26
Leutnant O. *Frhr.* von Beaulieu-Marconnay	25
Oberleutnant Robert Ritter von Greim	25
Leutnant Georg von Hantelmann	25
Leutnant Max Näther	25
Leutnant Fritz Pütter	25
Leutnant Erwin Böhme	24
Leutnant Hermann Becker	23
Leutnant Georg Meyer	23
Oberleutnant Hermann Goering	22
Leutnant Hans Klein	22
Leutnant Hans Pippart	22
Leutnant Werner Preuss	22
Vizefeldwebel Karl Schlegel	22
Leutnant Rudolph Windisch	22
Leutnant Hans Adam	21
Oberleutnant Friedrich Christiansen	21
Leutnant Fritz Friedrichs	21

	Victories
Leutnant Fritz Höhn	21
Vizefeldwebel Friedrich Altemeier	20
Oberleutnant Hans Bethge	20
Leutnant Rudolph von Eschwege	20
Leutnant Walter Goettsch	20
Leutnant Friedrich Noltenius	20
Hauptmann Wilhelm Reinhard	20

OTHER TOP ENEMY ACES, 1914–18

AUSTRO-HUNGARIAN

Like the British, the Austro-Hungarians considered only those with ten or more victories as aces. However, some thirty of their pilots downed more than five enemy aircraft apiece.

	Victories
Captain Godwin Brumowski	40
Lieutenant Julius Arigi	32
Lieutenant Frank Linke-Crawford	30
Lieutenant Benno Fiala	29
Lieutenant Josef Kiss	19

LEADING ALLIED ACES, 1914–18

FRENCH

There were a total of 160 aces in the French Aviation Service. Following are those who head the list:

	Victories
Captain René Fonck	75
Captain Georges Guynemer	53
Lieutenant Charles Nungesser	45
Lieutenant Georges Madon	41
Lieutenant Maurice Boyeau	35

AMERICAN

A total of 117 Americans shot down five or more enemy aircraft to become aces. This includes victories gained while serving with the French and British, but only those who eventually served in the U. S. Air Service are listed. Here are the first five:

	Victories
Captain Edward V. Rickenbacker	26
Lieutenant Frank Luke, Jr.	21
Major Raoul Lufbery	17
Lieutenant George A. Vaughn, Jr.	13
Captain Field E. Kindley	12

BRITISH

Some 550 British fighter pilots, including Commonwealth nations (Canada, Australia, New Zealand, Ireland, South Africa, etc.) downed five enemy aircraft each to qualify as aces. There were also nineteen Americans in their ranks. (Officially, the British did not recognize the designation, and in fact considered ten victories as the minimum.)

These are the top five:

	Victories
Major Edward "Mick" Mannock	~~73~~ 61
Lieutenant Colonel William A. Bishop	72
Major Raymond Collishaw	~~68~~ 60
Captain James B. McCudden	58
Captain A. Weatherby Beauchamp-Proctor	54

BELGIAN

Tiny Belgium produced a total of five aces:

	Victories
Lieutenant Willy Coppens	34
Lieutenant Edmond Thieffry	10
Adjutant André de Meulemeester	10
Captain Fernand Jacquet	7
Lieutenant Jan Olieslagers	6

ITALIAN

Among the forty-three Italian fliers who qualified as aces were:

	Victories
Major Francesco Baracca	36
Lieutenant Silvio Scaroni	26
Major Pier Ruggiero Piccio	24
Lieutenant Flavio Barracchini	21
Captain Fulco Ruffo di Calabria	20

RUSSIAN

Because of the Russian Revolution and the loss and destruction of official records, the total number of Russian aces will never be known. The following five head the list of those whose records remained or were reconstructed.

	Victories
Captain Alexander Kazakov	17
Captain P. d'Argueeff	15
Lieutenant Commander Alexander de Seversky	13
Lieutenant I. Smirnoff	12
Lieutenant M. Safonov	11

CHRONOLOGICAL SUMMARY OF THE WAR— WESTERN FRONT AND OTHER SIGNIFICANT DATES

1914

June

28—Archduke Francis Ferdinand, heir to throne of Austria-Hungary, assassinated at Sarajevo, Bosnia.

July

18—Aviation Section of the U. S. Army's Signal Corps authorized by Congress.

28—Austria-Hungary declares war on Serbia.

29—Russia mobilizes.

August

1—Germany declares war on Russia.

France mobilizes.

2—Germany invades Luxembourg.

3—Germany declares war on France.

4—Germany invades Belgium. Halted at Liege.

Great Britain at war with Germany.

5—President Wilson tenders good offices of United States in interests of peace.

6—Austria-Hungary at war with Russia.

7—French invade Alsace. Marshal Joffre in supreme command of French army.

Montenegro at war with Austria. British Expeditionary Force lands at Ostend, Calais, and Dunkirk.

8—Serbia at war with Germany.

Portugal announces readiness to stand by alliance with England.

12—France and Great Britain at war with Austria-Hungary.

Montenegro at war with Germany.

13–15—British RFC Squadrons fly to France.

17—Belgian capital removed from Brussels to Antwerp. Liege captured by Germans.

19—Canadian Parliament authorizes raising expeditionary force.

First RFC air reconnaissance patrol over the Western Front.

20—Germans occupy Brussels.

21—Battle of Charleroi.

22—RFC air reconnaissance patrol reports Von Kluck's enemy force advancing on British front.

23—British at Battle of Mons.

24—Germans enter France near Lille.

25—Three RFC planes force down first German aircraft.

26—Louvain sacked and burned by Germans. Viviani, Premiere of France.

28—Austria declares war on Belgium.

29—Russians invest Konigsberg, East Prussia.

30—Amiens occupied by Germans.

31—Russian army in East Prussia defeated at Tannenberg by Germans under Von Hindenburg.

September

3—Paris in state of siege; government transferred to Bordeaux.

4—Germans occupy Rheims.

6–10—Battle of Marne. Von Kluck beaten by Marshal Joffre. German army retreats from Paris to Soissons-Rheims line.

14—French reoccupy Amiens and Rheims.

20—Rheims cathedral shelled by Germans.

22—First British raid on German Zeppelin sheds in Dusseldorf and Cologne.

24—Allies occupy Peronne.

28—German aircraft first use black cross insignia.

29—Antwerp bombardment begins.

October

2—British Admiralty announces intention to mine North Sea areas.

8—British Naval aircraft destroy first Zeppelin in its shed at Dusseldorf.

9—Antwerp surrenders to Germans. Government removed to Ostend.

12—British aircraft on Western Front ordered to use national insignia.

13—British occupy Ypres.

14—Canadian Expeditionary Force of 32,000 men lands at Plymouth.

15—Germans occupy Ostend. Belgian government removed to Havre, France.

21—Zeppelin sheds at Friedrichshafen bombed.

December
14—First Battle of Champagne.
16—German squadron bombards Hartlepool, Scarborough, and Whitby on east coast of England.
25—British seaplanes raid Zeppelin sheds at Cuxhaven.

1915

January
Allied flier shoots down German plane with a rifle in the first aerial duel of the war.
First successful aerial photo reconnaissance.
Inception of artillery ranging and spotting from the air.

February
French Lieutenant Roland Garros downs enemy aircraft with fixed machine-gun firing between propeller blades.
10—Russians defeated by Germans in Battle of Masurian Lakes.
18—German submarines begin "blockade" of British Isles.
19–20—First German Zeppelin raid on England.

March
Anthony Fokker perfects synchronized machine gun.
10—British take Neuve-Chapelle in Flanders.
15—First merchant ship attacked from the air.

April
22—Second Battle of Ypres. Poison gas first used by Germans in attack on Canadians.
26—First Victoria Cross awarded for an air action.

May
7—*Lusitania,* Cunard liner, sunk by German submarine off Kinsale Head, Irish coast, with loss of 1152 lives; 102 Americans.
23—Italy declares war on Austria-Hungary and begins invasion on a 60-mile front.
31—German Zeppelin bombs London for first time (LZ. 38).

June
4–6—German aircraft bombs English towns.

7—RNAS Flight Sub-Lieutenant R. A. J. Warneford shoots down Zeppelin (LZ. 37) over Belgium.

The LZ. 38 destroyed in its shed at Evere.

15—Allied aircraft bombs Karlsruhe, in retaliation for raids on England.

July

11—RNAS airplanes do artillery spotting in sinking of *Konigsberg*.

31—Baden bombed by French aircraft.

August

12—First enemy ship torpedoed and sunk by British seaplane at the Dardanelles.

19—Colonel "Boom" Trenchard placed in command of the RFC in France.

September

25—Allies open Artois offensive and occupy Lens.

October

12—Edith Cavell, English nurse, shot by Germans for aiding British prisoners to escape from Belgium.

13—London bombed by Zeppelins; 55 persons killed; 114 injured.

14—Bulgaria at war with Serbia.

15—Great Britain declares war on Bulgaria.

17—France at war with Bulgaria.

19—Italy and Russia at war with Bulgaria.

29—Briand becomes Premiere of France, succeeding Viviani.

November

17—Anglo-French war council hold first meeting in Paris.

December

15—General Sir Douglas Haig succeeded Field Marshal Sir John French as Commander-in-Chief of British forces in France.

1916

January

Introduction of formation flying.

29–31—German Zeppelins bomb Paris and towns in England.

February

10—British conscription law goes into effect.

21—Battle of Verdun begins. Germans take Haumont.

25—Fort Douaumont falls to Germans.

March

9—Germany declares war on Portugal on the latter's refusal to give up seized ships.

15—Austria-Hungary at war with Portugal.

21—Escadrille Americaine, N. 124, authorized by French Air Service. (Later known as Lafayette Escadrille.)

31—Melancourt taken by Germans in Battle of Verdun.

April

French arm Nieuport 11s with Le Prieur air-to-air rockets. Successfully down Zeppelin.

14—RNAS planes bomb Constantinople (Istanbul) and Adrianople.

19—President Wilson publicly warns Germany not to pursue submarine policies.

20—Russian troops landed at Marseilles for service on French front.

Sergeant Eliott C. Cowdin, first American aviator awarded French *Medaille Militaire.*

May

15—Vimy Ridge gained by British.

22—French fighter pilots down 5 German observation balloons with Le Prieur rockets.

31—Battle of Jutland; British and German fleets engaged; heavy losses on both sides.

June

5—Kitchener, British Secretary of War, loses life when cruiser *Hampshire* is sunk off the Orkney Islands.

6—Germans capture Fort Vaux in Verdun attack.

18—First American shot down, H. Clyde Balsley of the Lafayette Escadrille.

July

1—British and French attack north and south of the Somme. RAF gains control of the air.

14—British Cavalry penetrate German second line.

15—Longueval captured by British.

25—Pozieres occupied by British.

30—British and French advance between Delville Wood and the Somme.

British and French air services carry out combined operations for first time.

August

3—French recapture Fleury.

27—Rumania declares war on Austria-Hungary.

28—Italy at war with Germany.

28—Germany at war with Rumania.

31—Bulgaria at war with Rumania. Turkey at war with Rumania.

September

2–3—Lieutenant W. Leefe Robinson first to shoot down Zeppelin over England.

15—British capture Flers-Courcelette, and other German positions on Western Front, using tanks directed from the air.

26—Combles and Thiepval captured by British and French.

October

1—Zeppelin L. 31 shot down near London.

24—Fort Douaumont recaptured by French.

November

2—Fort Vaux evacuated by Germans.

7—Woodrow Wilson re-elected President of the United States.

13—British advance along the Ancre.

22—Emperor Franz Josef of Austria-Hungary dies. Succeeded by Charles I.

23—German warships bombard English coast.

28—First German daylight air raid on London.

December

7—David Lloyd George succeeds Asquith as Prime Minister of England.

12—Approval for RAF to expand to 106 regular squadrons and 95 reserve squadrons.

15—French complete recapture of ground taken by Germans in Battle of Verdun.

18—President Wilson makes peace overtures to belligerents.

26—Germany replies to President's note and suggests a peace conference.

30—French government on behalf of Allies replies to President Wilson's note and refuses to discuss peace till Germany agrees to give "restitution, reparation, and guarantees."

1917

January

22—President Wilson suggests to the belligerents a "peace without victory."

31—Germany announces unrestricted submarine warfare.

February

3—United States severs diplomatic relations with Germany. Count Von Bernstorff is handed his passports.

17—British troops on the Ancre capture German positions.

28—United States makes public a communication from Germany to Mexico proposing an alliance, and offering as a reward the return of Mexico's lost territory in Texas, New Mexico, and Arizona (Zimmermann Telegram).

Submarine campaign of Germans results in the sinking of 134 vessels during February.

March

3—British advance on Bapaume.

4—Germans begin withdrawal along Hindenburg Line.

14—China breaks with Germany.

15—Czar Nicholas abdicates. Prince Lvoff heads new cabinet.

17—Bapaume falls to British. Roye and Lassigny occupied by French.

18—Peronne, Chaulnes, Nesle, and Noyon evacuated by Germans, who retreat on an eighty-five-mile front.

19—Alexander Ribot becomes French Premiere, succeeding Briand.

26–31—British advance on Cambrai.

April

6—United States declares war on Germany.

7—Cuba and Panama at war with Germany.

8—Austria-Hungary breaks with United States.

9—Germans retreat before British on long front (Battle of Arras).

9—Bolivia breaks with Germany.

13—Vimy, Givenchy, Bailleul, and positions about Lens taken by Canadians.

20—Turkey breaks with United States.

30—Major William C. Mitchell, first American officer to fly over the enemy lines.

May

7—German bombers make first night raid on London.

9—Liberia breaks with Germany.

15—Marshal Pétain succeeds Marshal Nivelle as Commander-in-Chief of French armies.

16—Bullecourt captured by British in the Battle of Arras.

17—Honduras breaks with Germany.

18—Conscription bill signed by President Wilson.

19—Nicaragua breaks with Germany.

20—British seaplane sinks first submarine from the air.

24—France asks U.S. to furnish 5000 pilots, 50,000 mechanics, and 4500 planes by spring 1918.

25—Twenty-one Gotha bombers make first mass daylight attack on England. 200 casualties.

26—Major T. F. Dodd appointed Aviation Officer on staff of Commander-in-Chief, AEF.

June

2—Aviation Section redesignated Airplane Division, Signal Corps.

5—Registration day for new draft army in United States.

7—Messines-Wytschaete ridge in English hands.

8—General John J. Pershing, Commander-in-Chief of American Expeditionary Forces, arrives in England en route to France.

13—588 casualties in first mass daylight raid on London by 14 Gothas.

18—Haiti breaks with Germany.

21—British War Office recommends expansion of RFC regular squadrons to 200.

30—Lieutenant Colonel Billy Mitchell replaces Major Dodd as Aviation Officer, American Expeditionary Forces (AEF).

July

1—Russians begin offensive in Gallicia. Kerensky, minister of war, leading in person.

3—AEF arrives in France.

4—First eight-cylinder Liberty engine, designed and built in six weeks, ready for testing.

6—Canadian House of Commons passes Compulsory Military Service Bill.

12—King Constantine of Greece abdicates in favor of his second son, Alexander.

16–23—Retreat of Russians on a front of 155 miles.

20—Drawing of draft numbers for American conscript army begins. Alexander Kerensky becomes Russian Premier, succeeding Lvoff.

22—Siam at war with Germany and Austria.

23—Major Benjamin D. Foulois appointed officer-in-charge Airplane Division.

24—$640 million appropriated to expand Airplane Division to 9989 officers and 87,083 men.

27—British DH 4 arrives in U.S. to serve as production model.

August

2—Sopwith Pup successfully landed on deck of H.M.S. *Furious*.

7—Liberia at war with Germany.

8—Canadian Conscription Bill passes its third reading in Senate.

13—First Aero Squadron leaves England to join AEF in France.

14—China at war with Germany and Austria-Hungary.

15—St. Quentin Cathedral destroyed by Germans.

15—Canadian troops capture Hill 70, dominating Lens.

21—Zeppelin destroyed off Danish coast by aircraft from H.M.S. *Yarmouth*.

22—Last German daylight air raid on England in World War I.

September

3—Brigadier General William L. Kenly becomes first Chief of Air Service, AEF.

5—New American National Army begins to assemble.

11—Guynemer killed.

14—Paul Painlevé becomes French Premier, succeeding Ribot.

16—Russia proclaimed a republic by Kerensky.

20—Costa Rica breaks with Germany.

26—Zonnebeke, Polygon Wood, and Tower Hamlets, east of
Ypres, taken by British.

October

1—Launch aircraft from H.M.S. *Repulse.*

6—Peru and Uruguay break with Germany.

9—Poelcapelle and other German positions captured in Franco-
British attack.

14—British form 41st Bomb Wing for strategic bombing of German industrial targets.

18—DH 4s ordered into mass production (4500 were built by the
end of the war, of which 1213 reached the front).

23—American troops in France fire their first shot in trench warfare.

French advance northeast of Soissons.

26—Brazil at war with Germany.

29—First American-built DH 4 flight tested at Dayton, Ohio.

November

1—Germans abandon position on Chemin des Dames.

3—Americans in trenches suffer twenty casualties in German
attacks.

6—Passchendaele captured by Canadians.

7—The Russian Bolsheviks, led by Lenin and Trotsky, seize Petrograd and depose Kerensky.

9—Italians retreat to the Piave.

10—Lenin becomes Premier of Russia, succeeding Kerensky.

15—Georges Clemenceau becomes Premier of France, succeeding
Painlevé.

20—Battle of Cambrai. Scout aircraft attack ground targets.

21—Ribecourt, Flesquieres, Havrincourt, Marcoing, and other
German positions captured by the British.

23—Italians repulse Germans on the whole front from the Asiago
Plateau to the Brenta River.

24—Battle of Cambrai. British tanks approach within three miles,
capturing Bourlon Wood.

27—Brigadier General B. D. Foulois replaces Brigadier General William L. Kenly as Chief of Air Service, AEF.

December

1—German East Africa reported completely conquered.

Allies' Supreme War Council, representing the United States, France, Great Britain, and Italy, holds first meeting at Versailles.

3—Russian Bolsheviks arrange armistice with Germans.

5—British retire from Bourlon Wood, Graincourt, and other positions west of Cambrai.

7—Finland declares independence.

8—Jerusalem, held by the Turks for 673 years, surrenders to British under General Edmund Allenby.

8—Ecuador breaks with Germany.

10—Panama at war with Austria-Hungary.

11—United States at war with Austria-Hungary.

15—Armistice signed between Germany and Russia at Brest-Litovsk.

17—Coalition government of Sir Robert Borden is returned and conscription confirmed in Canada.

26—The Curtiss JN-4 "Jenny" becomes basic trainer for American pilots.

1918

January

2—British Air Ministry formed.

3—Major General Sir Hugh Trenchard, first Chief of Air Staff.

8—President Wilson proclaimed his "Fourteen Points."

18—Major General Sir John Sâlmond succeeds Major General Sir Hugh "Boom" Trenchard as commander of the RFC in France.

19—American troops take over sector northwest of Toul.

20—Colonel Billy Mitchell, Chief of Air Service I Army Corps.

23—First AEF observation balloon ascends in France.

February

1—Argentine Minister of War recalls military attachés from Berlin and Vienna.

18—103rd Aero Squadron, AEF, made up of former members of the Lafayette Escadrille, begins operations at the front.

22—American troops in Chemin des Dames sector.

26—First U. S. Air Service unit to serve with American troops at the front was the 2nd Balloon Company.

March

1—Americans gain signal victory in salient north of Toul.

3—Peace treaty between Bolshevik government of Russia and the Central Powers signed at Brest-Litovsk.

4—Treaty signed between Germany and Finland.

5—Rumania signs preliminary treaty of peace with Central Powers.

7—First German bomber raid on London on a moonless night.

9—Russian capital moved from Petrograd to Moscow.

11—Lieutenant Paul Baer of the U. S. 103rd Aero Squadron awarded first Air Service Distinguished Service Cross.

14—Russo-German peace treaty ratified by All-Russian Congress of Soviets at Moscow.

Patrol by the U. S. 95th Aero Squadron constitutes first air action of the American 1st Pursuit Group.

19—Pilots of the 94th (Hat-in-the-Ring) Squadron fly first operational flights across the lines.

20—U. S. 28th Aero Squadron attached by flights to RAF squadrons in France.

21—Germans begin great drive on fifty-mile front from Arras to La Fere. Bombardment of Paris by German long-range gun from a distance of seventy-six miles.

24—Peronne, Ham, and Chauny evacuated by Allies.

25—Bapaume and Nesle occupied by Germans.

29—Marshal Ferdinand Foch chosen Commander-in-Chief of all Allied Armies on the Western Front.

April

1—The RFC and RNAS combined to form the Royal Air Force (RAF).

American Aviation Headquarters opened in Rome, Italy.

9—Second German drive begun in Flanders.

10—First German drive halted before Amiens after maximum advance of thirty-five miles.

11—First U.S. patrol over enemy lines in World War I, made by 1st Observation Group in two-seater Spads.

14—Lieutenant Douglas Campbell, 94th Aero Squadron, scores the first victory as an American trained pilot.

British Major General F. H. Sykes appointed Chief of Air Staff.

15—Second German drive halted before Ypres, after maximum advance of ten miles.

21—Guatemala at war with Germany.

Baron Manfred von Richthofen, ranking German flier, killed.

23—British naval forces raid German submarine base in Zeebrugge, Belgium, and block channel. First U.S. shipment of Liberty engines arrives in France.

27—Sir William Weir becomes Secretary of State for the RAF.

29—Lieutenant Edward V. Rickenbacker shoots down his first German plane.

May

7—Nicaragua at war with Germany and her allies.

11—First American-built DH 4 powered by a Liberty engine delivered to the AEF. First flight in France made on May 17.

19—Major Raoul Lufbery, famous American aviator, killed.

19–20—Last German bomber raid on England in which casualties were inflicted.

20—Army Aviation separated from the Signal Corps.

24—Costa Rica at war with Germany and Austria-Hungary.

Six HS-1s, American Navy-built seaplanes, first to arrive in France.

27—Third German drive begins on Aisne-Marne front of thirty miles between Soissons and Rheims.

28—Germans sweep on beyond Chemin des Dames and cross the Vesle at Fismes. Cantigny taken by Americans in local attack.

29—Soissons evacuated by French.

Brigadier General Mason M. Patrick becomes new Chief of Air Service, AEF.

31—Marne River crossed by Germans, who reached Château Thierry, forty miles from Paris.

June

3–6—American Marines and soldiers check advance of Germans at Château Thierry and Neuilly after maximum advance of Germans, thirty-two miles. Beginning of American co-operation on major scale.

5—Major General Sir Hugh Trenchard commands British Independent Air Force for strategic bombing of Germany.

9–14—German drive on Western Front ended.

12—First day U.S. day bombing by 96th Aero Squadron on railroad marshaling yards in France.

15–24—Austrian drive on Italian front ends in complete failure.

30—American troops in France number 1,019,115.

July

1—Vaux taken by Americans.

3—Mohammed V, Sultan of Turkey, dies.

8—Sopwith Camels from the aircraft carrier *Furious* destroy Zepplins L. 54 and L. 60.

10—Czechoslovaks, aided by Allies, take control of a long stretch of the Trans-Siberian Railway.

15—Haiti at war with Germany.

15—Defense of Château Thierry blocks new German drive on Paris.

17—Lieutenant Quentin Roosevelt, youngest son of ex-President Theodore Roosevelt, killed in aerial battle near Château Thierry.

18—French and Americans begin counter offensive on Marne-Aisne front.

20—U. S. 148th Aero Squadron begins operation with the RAF near Dunkirk.

23—French take Oulchy-le-Château and drive the Germans back ten miles between the Aisne and the Marne.

30—Allies astride the Ourcq; Germans in full retreat to the Vesle.

August

1—Sergeant Joyce Kilmer, American poet and critic, aged thirty-one, dies in battle with the U. S. "Fighting 69th" Regiment.

2—French troops recapture Soissons.

18 U.S. built DH 4s with Liberty engines fly their first patrol along the front.

3—President Wilson announces new policy regarding Russia and agrees to co-operate with Great Britain, France, and Japan in sending forces to Murmansk, Archangel, and Vladivostok.

3—Allies sweep on between Soissons and Rheims, driving the enemy from his base at Fismes and capturing the entire Aisne-Vesle front.

5—Last Zeppelin raid on England. L. 70 shot down.

7—Franco-American troops cross the Vesle.

8—New Allied drive begun by British Field-Marshal Haig in Picardy, penetrating enemy front fourteen miles.

10—Montdidier recaptured.

11—Sopwith Camel launched from towed lighter shoots down Zeppelin L. 53.

13—Lassigny *massif* taken by French.

15—Canadians capture Damery and Parvillers, northwest of Roye.

21—Battle of Bapaume.

26—Battle of the Scarpe.

28—Battle of the Somme (1918).

29—Noyon and Bapaume fall in new Allied advance.

September

1—Australians take Peronne.

Americans fight for the first time on Belgian soil and capture Voormezeele.

11—Germans are driven back to the Hindenburg Line, which they held in November 1917.

12—Registration day for new U.S. draft of men between eighteen and forty-five.

Lieutenant Frank Luke, the American "Balloon Buster" of the 27th Aero Squadron, scores his first victory.

13—Americans begin vigorous offense in St. Mihiel Sector on forty-mile front. A total of 1481 Allied planes under command of Brigadier General Billy Mitchell, largest air armada ever assembled, participated in the offensive.

14—St. Mihiel recaptured from Germans. General Pershing announces entire St. Mihiel salient erased, liberating more than 150 square miles of French territory that had been in German hands since 1914.

19–20—RFC destroys Turkish Seventh Army in Palestine from the air.

25—British take forty thousand prisoners in Palestine offensive.

Lieutenant E. V. Rickenbacker attacks seven enemy planes. He later received the Medal of Honor for this exploit.

27—Franco-Americans in drive from Rheims to Verdun take thirty thousand prisoners.

Begin attack on Hindenburg Line.

28—Belgians attack enemy from Ypres to North Sea, gaining four miles.

29—Bulgaria surrenders to General Franchet d'Esperey, the Allied commander.

30—British-Belgian advance reaches Roulers.

October

1—St. Quentin, cornerstone of Hindenburg Line, captured.

Allies bomb Germans using electrical bomb release for first time.

Damascus occupied by British in Palestine campaign.

2—Lens evacuated by Germans. The United States "Bug," guided missile, successfully flight tested at Dayton.

3—Albania cleared of Austrians by Italians.

4—King Ferdinand of Bulgaria abdicates; Boris succeeds.

5—Prince Maximilian, new German Chancellor, pleads with President Wilson to ask Allies for armistice.

7—Berry-au-Bac taken by French.

9—Cambrai in Allied hands.

11—Americans advance through Argonne forest.

12—German foreign secretary, Solf, says plea for armistice is made in name of German people; agrees to evacuate all foreign soil.

American pursuit pilots participate in first U.S. night air fighter action.

13—Laon and La Fere abandoned by Germans.

Grandpre captured by Americans after four days' battle.

14—President Wilson refers Germans to Marshall Foch for armistice terms.

A British Handley-Page drops a 1650-pound bomb, largest of the war.

16—Lille entered by British patrols.

17—Ostend, German submarine base, taken by land and sea forces.

Douai falls to Allies.

19—Bruges and Zeebrugge taken by Belgian and British forces.

25—Beginning of terrific Italian drive, which nets fifty thousand prisoners in five days.

26—"Boom" Trenchard appointed Commander-in-Chief, Inter-Allied Independent Air Force.

31—Turkey surrenders; armistice takes effect at noon; conditions include free passage of Dardanelles.

November

1—Clery-le-Grand captured by American First Army troops.

3—Americans sweep ahead on fifty-mile front above Verdun; enemy in full retreat. German Fleet mutinies at Kiel.

Official reports announce capture of 362,350 Germans since 3 P.M. after five hundred thousand prisoners had been taken.

4—Americans advance beyond Stenay and strike at Sedan.

Victory of Vittorio Veneto.

7—American "Rainbow" Division and parts of 1st Division enter suburbs of Sedan.

8—Heights south of Sedan seized by Americans.

9—Maubeuge captured by Allies.

10—Canadians take Mons in irresistible advance.

The 3rd Pursuit Group flies last American patrol over enemy lines.

11—Germany surrenders; armistice takes effect at 11 A.M. American flag hoisted on Sedan front.

SPECIFICATIONS AND DATA OF SELECTED AIRCRAFT TYPES FLOWN BY UDET

Albatros D III

Single-seater scout of early 1917, one of the most successful of its line. It replaced the earlier excellent D I and D II of 1916. The D III was itself replaced later in 1917 by the D V, which resembled it closely in physical appearance.

Engine — 175-hp. Mercedes
Wingspan — 29 ft., 7 ins.
Length — 24 ft., 2 ins.
Weight — 2050 lbs. loaded
Speed — 120 m.p.h. at sea level
Armament — 2 fixed Spandau machine guns

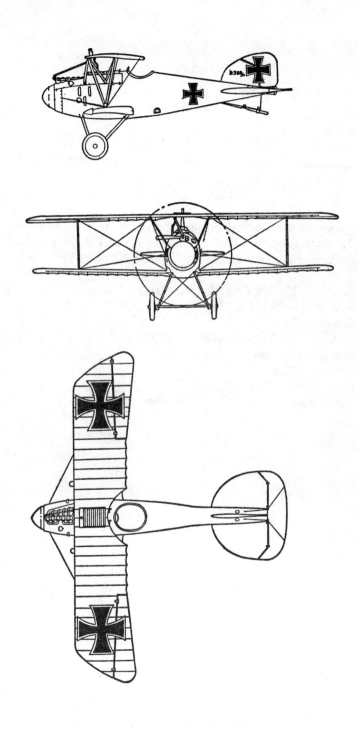

Fokker Eindekker III

Single-seater scout or fighter, appeared at the front in December 1915. Its predecessor, Model E I, was the first to have a fixed machine gun synchronized to fire between the propeller blades.

Engine — 100-hp. Oberursel rotary
Wingspan — 31 ft., 3 ins.
Length — 24 ft.
Weight — 1400 lbs. loaded
Speed — 83 m.p.h. at 6500 ft.
Ceiling — 11,000 ft.
Endurance — 2 hrs., 45 mins.
Armament — 1 fixed Spandau machine gun

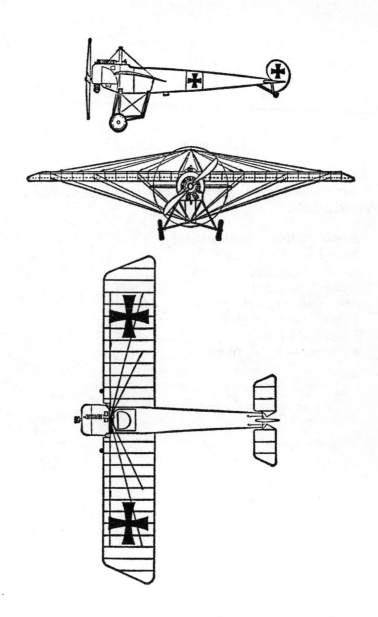

Fokker Dr I Triplane

Single-seater scout arrived on the Western Front in August 1917.
It was a small, highly maneuverable triplane favored by Voss and
von Richthofen.

Engine — 110-hp. Oberursel rotary
Wingspan — 23 ft., 7 ins.
Speed — 122 m.p.h. at 8900 ft.
Ceiling — 20,000 ft.
Armament — 2 fixed Spandau machine guns
Weight — 1289 lbs. gross
Length — 19 ft.
Endurance — 2 hrs., 30 mins.

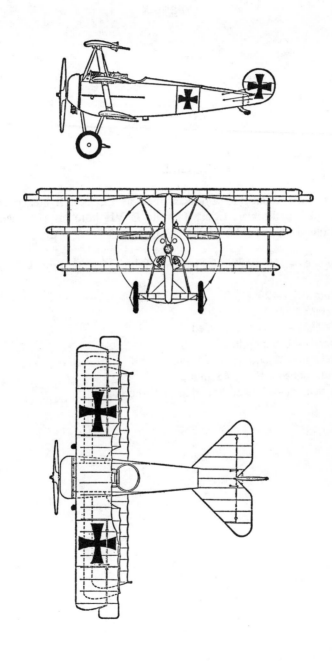

Fokker D VII

Single-seater scout (1918), acclaimed as the best fighter plane developed in the war. Udet's favorite D VII bore his girl friend Lo's name on the sides of the fuselage.

Engine — 160-, 180-, 200-, or 220-hp. Mercedes; or 185-hp.
B.M.W.
Wingspan — 29 ft., 3½ ins.
Length — 23 ft.
Weight — 1960 lbs. loaded
Speed — 135 m.p.h. (220 hp.)
Ceiling — 22,000 ft. (185 hp.)
Endurance — 1 hr., 45 mins.
Armament — 2 fixed Spandau machine guns

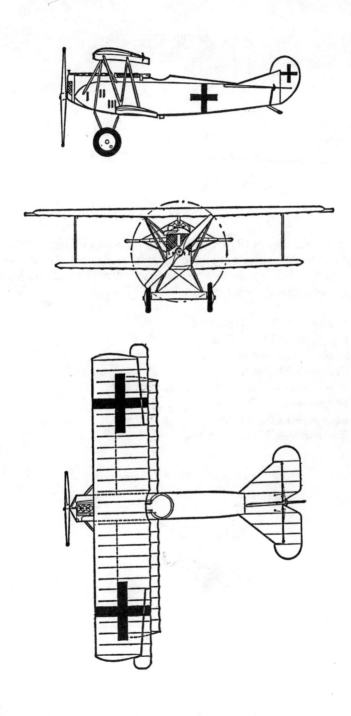

Fokker D VIII

Single-seater scout (1918). This last in the series of World War I
Fokker fighters might have been the best in its line. It came out
late in October, barely two weeks before the close of the war.
Udet, who flew it, called it the "Parasol" Fokker.

Engine — 140-hp. Oberursel
Wingspan — 27 ft., 3 ins.
Speed — 125 m.p.h.
Ceiling — 21,000 ft.
Armament — 2 fixed Spandau machine guns
Weight — 1331 lbs. loaded
Length — 19 ft., 5 ins.
Endurance — 1 hr., 30 mins.

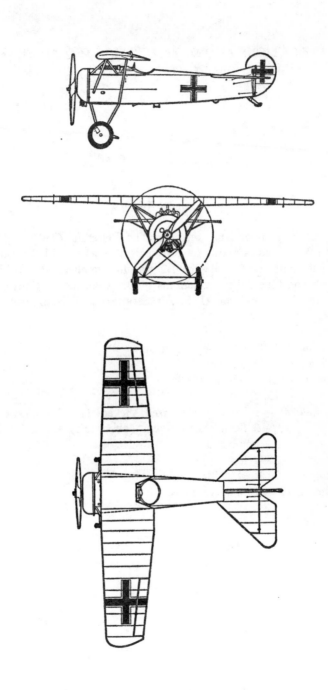

SPECIFICATIONS AND DATA OF SELECTED AIRCRAFT
TYPES BROUGHT DOWN BY UDET

Breguet 14

Two-seater bomber and reconnaissance aircraft (1917). The model A2 served primarily for reconnaissance and could also carry a small bomb load, while the B2 was the bomber version. The French had ninety-three squadrons of Breguets, the Belgians had two squadrons, and the U. S. Air Service had 366 Breguets in 1918.

Engine — 220- or 300-hp. Renault
Wingspan — 48 ft., 9 ins.
Speed — 121 m.p.h. at sea level
Ceiling — 19,000 ft.
Armament — 1 fixed synchronized Vickers (pilot's) and 2 or 3 flexible Lewis guns* (observer's) and a 520-lb. bomb load.
Weight — 3891 lbs.
Length — 29 ft., 1¼ ins.
Endurance — 2 hrs., 45 mins.

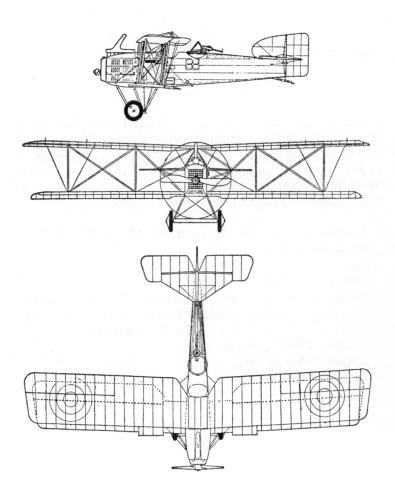

Bristol Fighter F2b

Two-seater fighter and reconnaissance aircraft (1916). The "Bris-fit" was one of the better airplanes developed during the war. Four of a flight of six Bristol F2a's went down before the onslaught of von Richthofen's *staffel* at the Battle of Arras, following which the Bristol Fighter was considered a "jinx." A later change of tactics, however, made it a most formidable fighter.

Engine — 200-hp. Sunbeam Arab or 200-hp. Hispano-Suiza
Wingspan — 39 ft., 3 ins.
Speed — 120 m.p.h. at sea level
Ceiling — 20,000 ft.
Armament — 1 fixed Vickers (pilot's) and 1 or 2 flexible
Lewis guns on Scarff mount in rear (observer's).
It could carry a 240-lb. bomb load.
Weight — 2630 lbs. loaded
Length — 24 ft., 9 ins.
Endurance — 3 hrs.

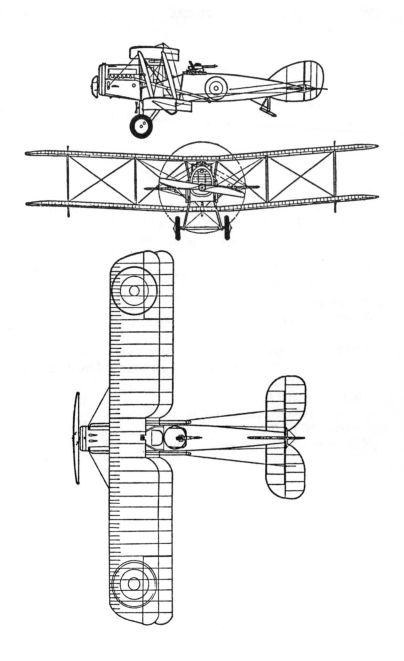

Bristol Scout "Bullet"

Single-seater designed primarily for reconnaissance (1914) but was later armed as a fighter. McCudden called it "a most excellent flying machine, and quite easy to fly and land."

Engine — 80- or 100-hp. Gnôme; 80- or 110-hp. Le Rhône; 130-hp. Clerget

Wingspan — 24 ft., 5 ins.

Speed — 98 m.p.h. at sea level (80 hp.); 104 m.p.h. at sea level (100 hp.)

Armament — None when they first came out, but late in 1915 they were fitted with 1 synchronized fixed Vickers gun.

Ceiling — 15,500 ft. (80 hp.)

Weight — 1195 lbs. loaded (80 hp.)

Length — 20 ft., 7 ins.

Endurance — 2 hrs., 30 mins.

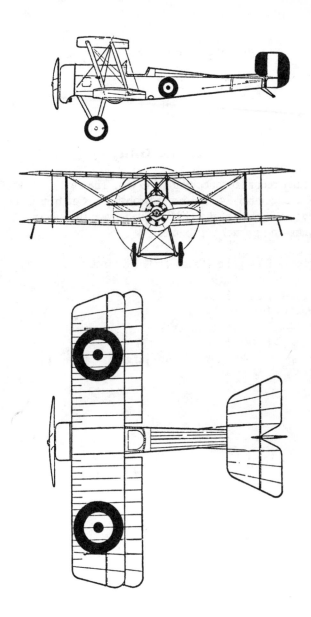

Caudron G III

Two-seater reconnaissance plane (1915). The aircraft downed by Udet on December 24, 1916 was probably a Caudron G IV, the twin-engine version of the G III. It had twice the power, a longer wingspan, and greater capabilities.

Engine — 80-hp. Le Rhône or Gnôme rotary
Wingspan — 43 ft., 9 ins.
Length — 22 ft., 6 ins.
Weight — 1619 lbs. loaded
Speed — 70 m.p.h. at sea level
Ceiling — 10,000 ft.
Armament — None, except for sidearms carried by the crew.

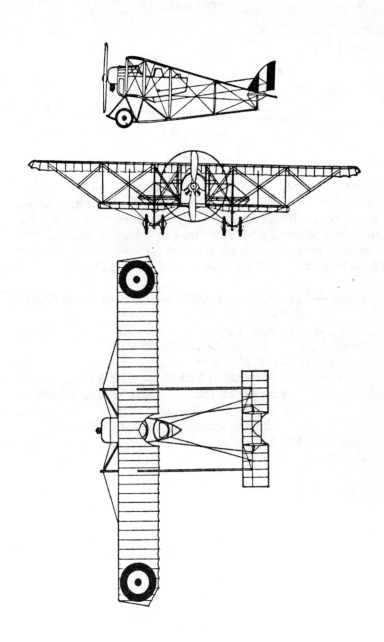

DH 4

Two-seater bomber and reconnaissance aircraft (1917). Designed by Geoffrey de Havilland as a high-speed day bomber, it served with RFC and RNAS squadrons in 1917. However, more of them were built in the United States than in Britain. It was the only American-built aircraft to see action at the front and was the type flown by Lieutenant Wanamaker when Udet shot him down.

Engine — 250- or 375-hp. Rolls-Royce, or the American 400-hp. Liberty 12

Wingspan — 42 ft., 4½ ins.

Speed — 143 m.p.h. at sea level (375 hp.)

Ceiling — 22,000 ft. (375 hp.)

Armament — 1 synchronized Vickers for pilot, 2 flexible Lewis guns in the rear. American models substituted twin Browning or Marlin machine guns for the Vickers. It could carry 350 lbs. of bombs.

Weight — 3472 lbs. loaded

Length — 30 ft., 8 ins.

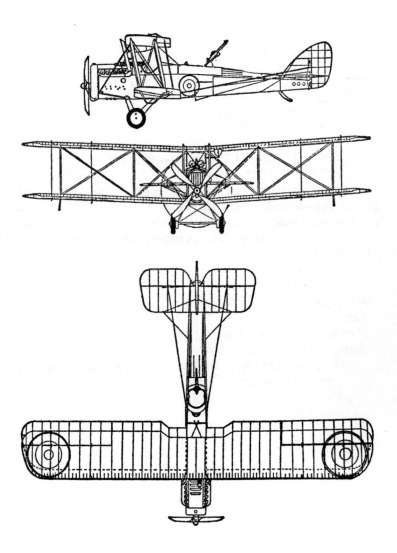

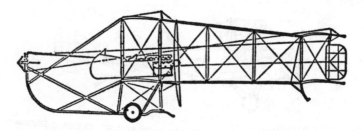

Maurice Farman "Longhorn"

Two-seater French-designed and -built reconnaissance and training aircraft (prewar). The first aircraft shot down by Udet was a Farman, and although he doesn't describe it in detail, it was probably in the F 20 or F 40 series rather than the "Longhorn" or "Shorthorn."

Engine — 70-hp. Renault
Wingspan — 58 ft., 8 ins.
Length — 32 ft.
Weight — 1887 lbs. loaded
Speed — 59 m.p.h. at sea level
Armament — None except for rifle or pistol carried by pilot and/
       or observer.

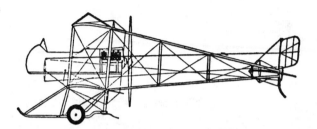

Maurice Farman "Shorthorn"

Two-seater reconnaissance and bomber aircraft (prewar). The "Shorthorn" was an improved version of the "Longhorn." It appeared at the front in 1915, a year after its predecessor, and served with the Russian and Italian air forces as well as the French.

Engine — 70-hp. Renault
Wingspan — 53 ft.
Length — 30 ft., 8 ins.
Weight — 2046 lbs. loaded
Speed — 66 m.p.h. at sea level
Endurance — 3 hrs., 45 mins.
Armament — None except for rifles or pistols carried by crew.

Nieuport 11

Single-seater scout (1915). Nicknamed *bébé,* or "baby," because of its small size, it became the French answer to the Fokker Eindekker. The *bébé* was very popular with the French squadrons and with the Americans of the Lafayette Escadrille.

Engine — 80-hp. Gnôme Monosoupape or Le Rhône Rotary
Wingspan — 24 ft., 6 ins.
Speed — 97 m.p.h.
Ceiling — 15,000 ft.
Armament — 1 flexible Lewis gun mounted on top wing.
Weight — 1210 lbs. loaded
Length — 19 ft.
Endurance — 2 hrs., 30 mins.

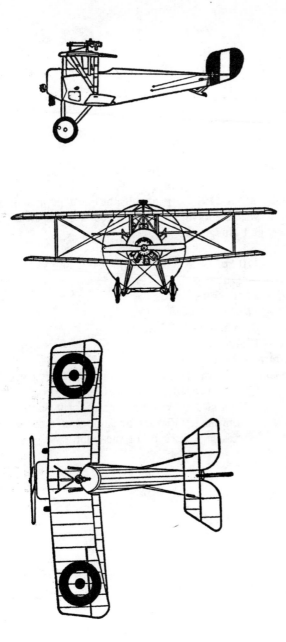

Nieuport 17

Single-seater scout (1916). Probably the most popular fighter of the war. It was the favorite of such top aces as Bishop, Ball, Guynemer, and Nungesser.

Engine — 110-hp. Le Rhône rotary
Wingspan — 27 ft.
Length — 19 ft., 6 ins.
Weight — 1233 lbs. loaded
Speed — 107 m.p.h. at 6500 ft.
Ceiling — 17,400 ft.
Endurance — 2 hrs.
Armament — 1 Lewis gun mounted on upper wing which fired over propeller and could be raised or lowered but not swung from side to side, or a single fixed synchronized Vickers machine gun mounted on the fuselage forward of the pilot.

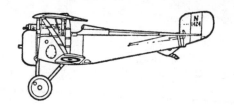

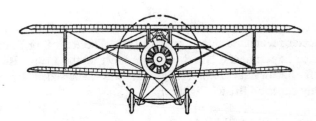

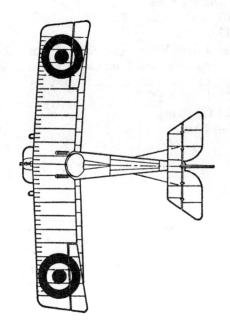

R.E. 8

Two-seater reconnaissance aircraft (1916). The R.E. 8 or Reconnaissance Experimental No. 8 was a product of the British Royal Aircraft Factory at Farnborough. It was superseded by the infinitely superior Bristol Fighter.

Engine — 150-hp. RAF 4a
Wingspan — 42 ft., 7 ins.
Speed — 102 m.p.h. at 6500 ft.
Ceiling — 13,000 ft.
Armament — 1 fixed Vickers (pilot's) and 1 or 2 flexible Lewis guns on Scarff mounting (observer's). It could carry a 260-lb. bomb load.
Weight — 2678 lbs. loaded
Length — 27 ft., 10 ins.
Endurance — 4 hrs., 30 mins.

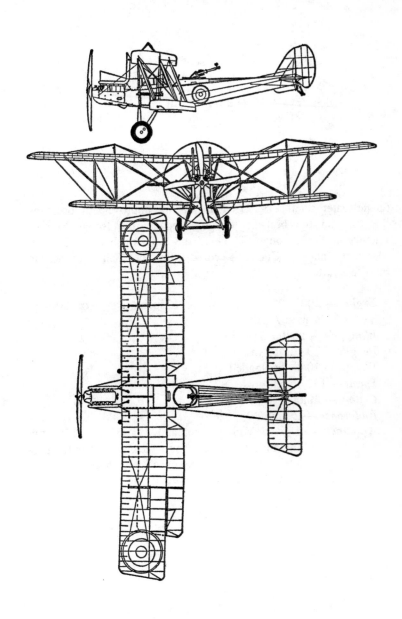

S.E. 5A

Single-seater scout (1917). This was an improvement over the S.E. 5, and the best fighter produced by the Royal Aircraft Factory at Farnborough. Three of the top British aces—Bishop, Mannock, and McCudden—scored most of their victories in these aircraft.

Engine — 200-, 220-, or 240-hp. Hispano-Suiza; or 200-hp. Wolseley Viper

Wingspan — 26 ft., 7½ ins.

Length — 20 ft., 11 ins.

Weight — 2048 lbs. loaded

Speed — 132 m.p.h.

Ceiling — 20,000 ft.

Endurance — 2 hrs., 30 mins.

Armament — 1 fixed Vickers gun, and 1 Lewis machine gun mounted on upper wing which fired over the propeller and could be raised or lowered but not swung from side to side.

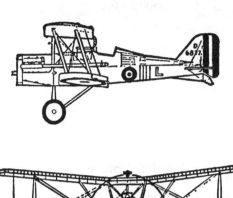

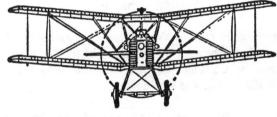

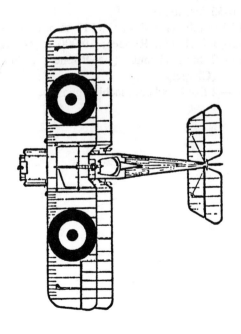

Sopwith Camel F 1

Single-seater scout (1917). More enemy aircraft were destroyed by this British fighter than by any other in the First World War. It was flown by Canadian Captain Roy Brown in the action in which Von Richthofen was shot down.

Engine — 110-hp. Le Rhône rotary or 130-hp. Clerget rotary
Wingspan — 28 ft.
Length — 18 ft., 8 ins.
Weight — 1453 lbs. loaded
Speed — 119 m.p.h. (Le Rhône); 113 m.p.h. (Clerget)
Ceiling — 24,000 ft. (Le Rhône); 19,000 ft. (Clerget)
Endurance — 2 hrs., 45 min. (Le Rhône); 2 hrs., 30 min. (Clerget)
Armament — 2 fixed Vickers machine guns

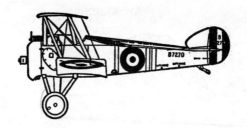

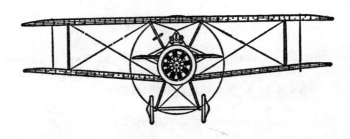

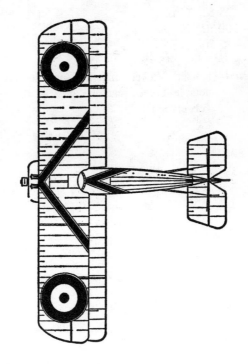

Sopwith 1½ Strutter

Two-seater British-designed reconnaissance and bomber aircraft, most likely the aircraft brought down by Udet on August 15, 1917. He described it as a "Sopwith two-seater."

Engine — 110-hp. or 130-hp. Clerget rotary
Wingspan — 33 ft., 6 ins.
Length — 25 ft., 3 ins.
Speed — 100 m.p.h.
Ceiling — 15,500 ft.
Endurance — 3 hrs., 45 mins.
Armament — 1 fixed Vickers machine gun forward, and one flexible Lewis machine gun in the rear cockpit (observer's).

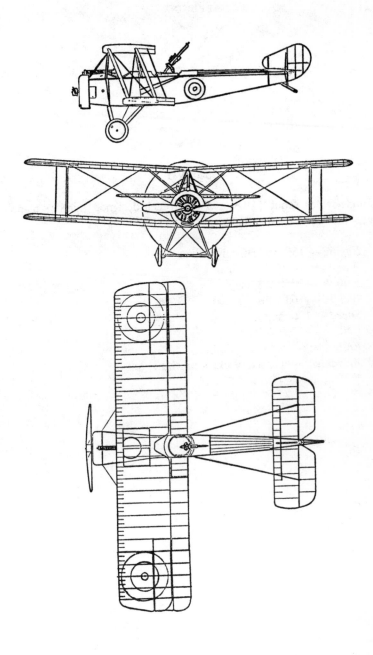

Spad VII

Single-seater scout (1916). This French-designed fighting plane was also used by the RFC.

Engine — 150-hp. Hispano-Suiza
Wingspan — 25 ft., 8 ins.
Length — 20 ft., 3 ins.
Weight — 1632 lbs. loaded
Speed — 120 m.p.h.
Ceiling — 17,500 ft.
Endurance — 2 hrs., 30 mins.
Armament — 1 fixed Vickers machine gun

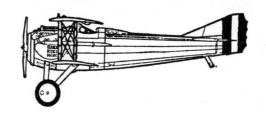

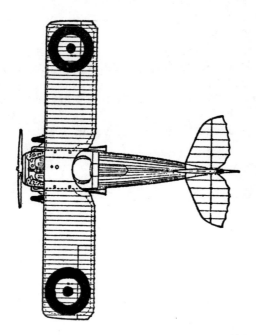

Spad XIII

Single-seater scout (1917). It was the principal aircraft of the American pursuit squadrons and the French Aviation Militaire at the end of the war.

Engine — 220-hp. Hispano-Suiza (1917) or 235-hp. Hispano-Suiza (1918)
Wingspan — 26 ft., 4 ins.
Length — 20 ft., 8 ins.
Weight — 1807 lbs. loaded
Speed — 134 m.p.h. (220 hp.); 139 m.p.h. (235 hp.)
Ceiling — 22,300 ft.
Endurance — 1 hr., 40 min. (220 hp.); 4 hrs., 30 mins. (235 hp.)
Armament — 2 fixed Vickers machine guns

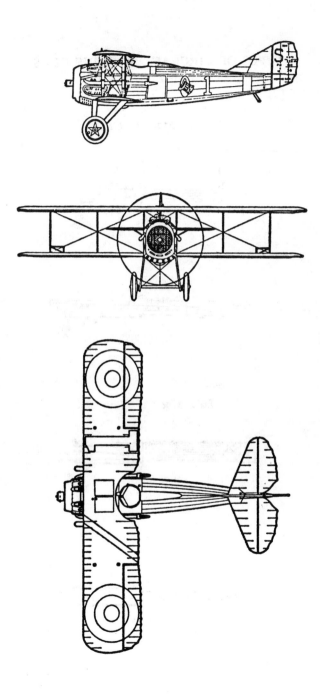

TYPES OF AIRCRAFT MACHINE GUNS
OF WORLD WAR I

ALLIED

Flexible Machine Guns

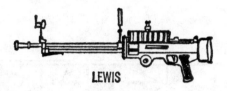

LEWIS

HOTCHKISS

Fixed Machine Guns

VICKERS

BROWNING

GERMAN

Flexible Machine Gun

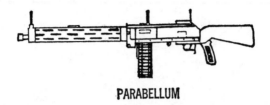

PARABELLUM

Fixed Machine Gun

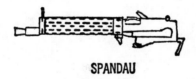

SPANDAU